DEAR FRIEND:

Trees shade and cool our homes, bring songbirds close by, and mark the changing seasons. Children can climb them or build a tree house in their branches. For all of us trees are a source of lumber, food, and countless products—and they beautify our communities and the countryside.

But equally important, trees keep our water clean, reduce soil erosion, clean the air we breathe, and fight global warming.

If trees are to provide all these benefits, we need to care for the trees we have and plant more. Planting and caring for trees is something each of us can do to improve our community and help the environment.

If we are to have trees in abundance, it is important to be able to identify them so we will know how to care for them and plant the right trees in the right place.

And it's just plain fun to be able to identify trees, either those in your neighborhood or on a trip far from home.

To help you learn to identify trees, the Arbor Day Foundation has prepared this key for your use.

I hope you will use this guide regularly to help you appreciate trees—one of nature's great wonders.

Best regards,

John Rosenow

John Rosenow
Chief Executive

Arbor Day Foundation®

Arbor Day Foundation
211 N. 12th Street
Lincoln, NE 68508
www.arborday.org

First printing 2009

Printed in Canada

LIBRARY OF CONGRESS CATALOGING-IN-PUBLICATION DATA

ISBN: 978-0-9634657-5-7

What Tree Is That?
Category 1: Nature Category 2: Garden
LCCN: #2008939816

Table of Contents

HOW TO USE THIS BOOK

This book is intended to be used as a field guide to assist you in identifying trees by their leaves. In some cases, fruiting bodies, seeds, bark or other parts are helpful in making an identification.

1. Examine several leaves or needles from the same tree. Choose typical ones to identify. Avoid choosing oddities or rarities. Also observe fruiting bodies, flowers, seeds, and bark.

2. Beginning on page 6 with Box 6A, there is a series of questions about the leaves and other tree parts. Each answer leads to another question until the identity of the tree is discovered.

Each featured tree is listed alphabetically in the index, pages 142–148, for quick reference. The words printed in CAPITAL LETTERS are defined in context when they first appear and in alphabetical order in the Glossary on the inside flap.

ARBOR DAY HARDINESS ZONES

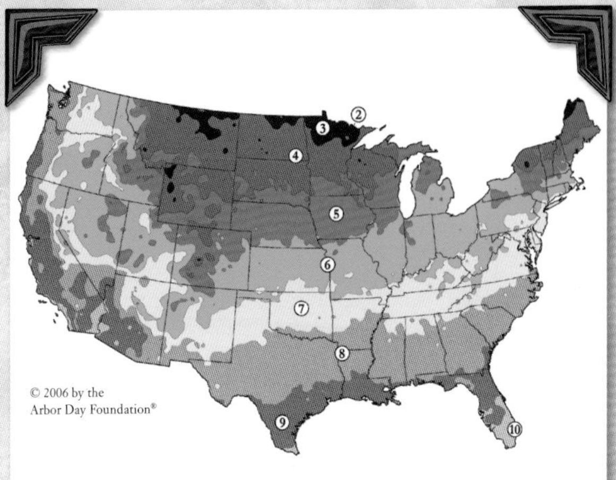

Go to arborday.org
to find the zone for your zip code.

Zone	Avg. Annual Low
2	-40°F through -50°F
3	-30°F through -40°F
4	-20°F through -30°F
5	-10°F through -20°F
6	0°F through -10°F
7	10°F through 0°F
8	20°F through 10°F
9	30°F through 20°F
10	40°F through 30°F

It is helpful to know where in the country a tree is most likely to grow. Hardiness zones in the U.S. are noted with the leaf art for each species. For example, zones 4-9 means that a tree is "hardy" in zones 4, 5, 6, 7, 8, and 9, according to the arborday.org Hardiness Zone map above, based on the most recently compiled average annual minimum temperatures recorded by U.S. weather stations. Suitable hardiness means a tree can be expected to grow in the zone's temperature range. However, local variations such as moisture, soil, winds, and other conditions might affect a tree's adaptability to a particular locale.

Trees Identified in This Book

This tree key was written for use in the colored area in the United States and Canada. Only the more common trees are identified. Cultivars (special selections of a species), uncommon species, and palm trees have not been included.

HOW TO USE THIS KEY:

1. In each box there are two or more questions. Each yes answer is followed by a GO TO direction which indicates a page number and box identifier.
2. Read each question in the box. Follow the directions by the question most correctly answered yes, moving to the page and box number indicated.
3. By repeating this process and turning to the pages indicated, the yes answer will direct you to the box that names the tree. The color of the YES GO TO box will match the color of the tree's box identifier. Compare the leaf drawing with your leaf sample.

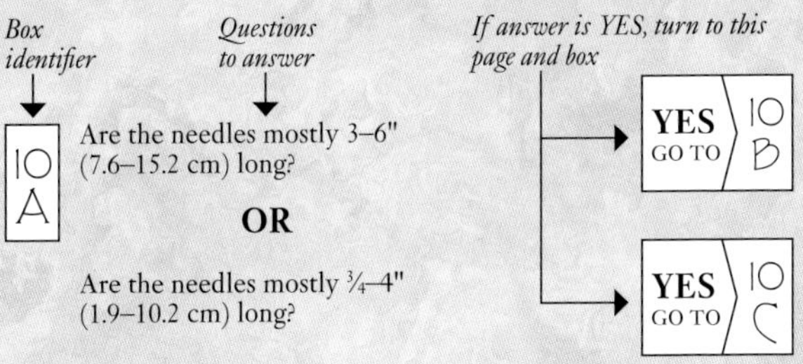

If you have some idea about the tree's name, you may also look it up in the index, which lists the page where each species is shown.

START HERE

5 A

Do you live east of the Rocky Mountains or in the blue shaded area of Canada or Alaska?

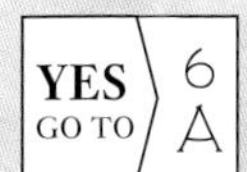

OR

Do you live west of the Rocky Mountains or in the green shaded area of Canada or Alaska?

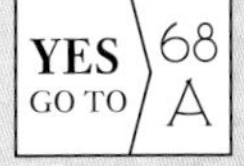

EASTERN START HERE

6A

Does the tree bear cones and have leaves that are needle-like? **CLUE:** *These trees are called CONIFERS (cone-bearing) and most are EVERGREEN (tree with needles or leaves that remain alive and on the tree through the winter and into the next growing season).*

YES GO TO 7D

OR

Does the tree bear cones that are sometimes berry-like and have leaves that hug the twig and are scale-like or awl-shaped? **CLUE:** *These trees are called CONIFERS (cone-bearing) and most are EVERGREEN.*

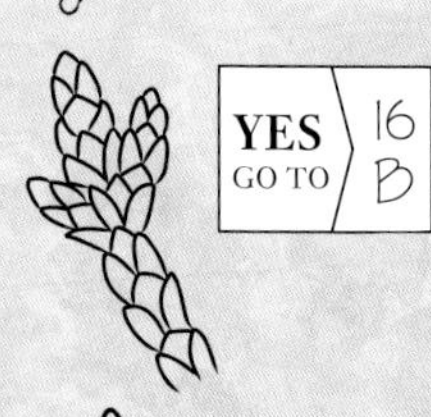

YES GO TO 16B

OR

Does the tree have leaves that are flat and thin? **CLUE:** *These trees are called BROADLEAF, (a tree with leaves that are flat and thin) and bear a variety of fruit and flowers. Most are DECIDUOUS (shedding all leaves annually).*

YES GO TO 7A

7A

Are the leaves SIMPLE (one BLADE attached to a stalk or PETIOLE)?

YES GO TO **7B**

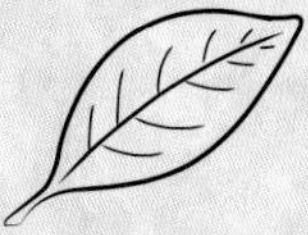

OR

Are the leaves COMPOUND (more than one BLADE attached to a single stalk or PETIOLE)?

YES GO TO **7C**

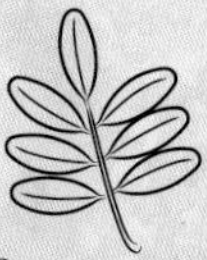

OR

Are the uniquely fan-shaped leaves mostly attached, in clusters, to short, SPUR-like branches? It is a **ginkgo.**

YES GO TO **25B**

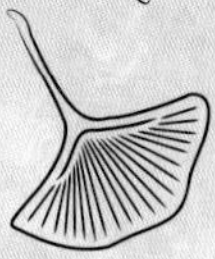

7B

Are the SIMPLE leaves OPPOSITE (2 leaves that are directly across from each other on the same twig)?

YES GO TO **18A**

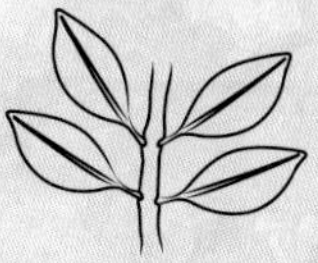

OR

Are the SIMPLE leaves ALTERNATE (leaves that are staggered, not opposite each other on the twig)?

YES GO TO **24B**

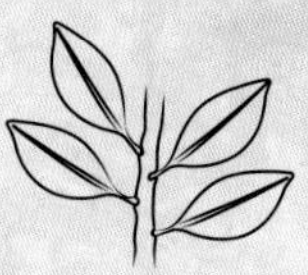

7C

Are the COMPOUND leaves OPPOSITE?

YES GO TO **20D**

OR

Are the COMPOUND leaves ALTERNATE?

YES GO TO **58B**

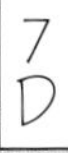

7D

Are the trees EVERGREEN with needles arranged in clusters of 2–5? These are pine trees.

YES GO TO **8A**

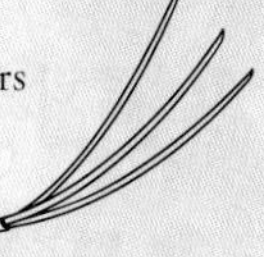

OR

Are the trees DECIDUOUS, with needles arranged in clusters of many on short, SPUR-like branches? These are larches.

YES GO TO **12A**

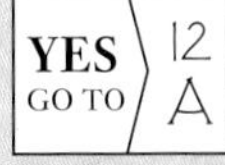

OR

Are the trees EVERGREEN with needles arranged singly?

YES GO TO **12B**

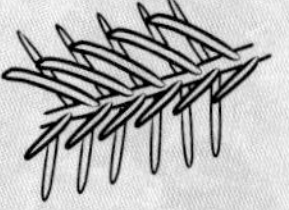

OR

Are the trees DECIDUOUS with singly attached needles of uneven length flattened along the twig, the cone a 1" (2.5 cm) diameter green or brown wrinkled ball? It is a **baldcypress.**

YES GO TO **14D**

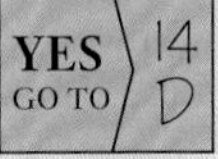

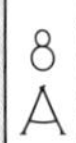

Are the needles clustered in groups of 5 and the cones long with thin scales? It is an **eastern white pine.**

YES GO TO 9A

OR

Are the needles clustered in groups of 2 or 3, and the cone scales thick and often tipped with spines?

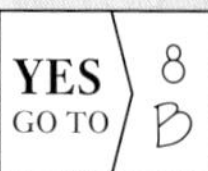

Are the needles clustered in groups of 3?

YES GO TO 8C

OR

Are the needles clustered in groups of 2?

OR

Are the needles clustered in groups of 2 and 3 on the same tree?

Are the needles 3–5" (7.6–12.7 cm) long, somewhat twisted, often sprouting in tufts from the trunk; cones 2–3½" (5.1–8.9 cm) long? It is a **pitch pine.**

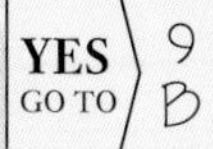

OR

Are the needles 8–18" (20.3–45.7 cm) long, cones 6–10" (15.2–25.4 cm) long? It is a **longleaf pine.**

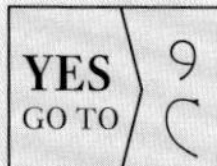

OR

Are the needles 6–9" (15.2–22.9 cm) long, cones 3–6" (7.6–15.2 cm) long? It is a **loblolly pine.**

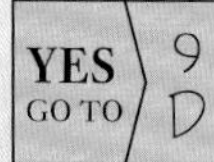

9A Eastern White Pine

Pinus strobus
Zones 3–8

The fabled tree eagerly sought by the first wave of loggers in America. The provincial tree of Ontario.

9B Pitch Pine

Pinus rigida
Zones 4–7

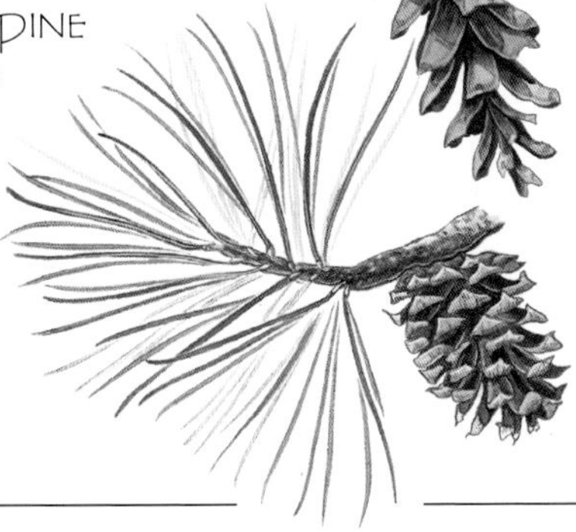

The fire resilient conifer of the East, even producing new branches and needles after fire kills the green foliage

9C Longleaf Pine

Pinus palustris
Zones 7–10

A tall, stately pine of the South long sought by loggers

9D Loblolly Pine

Pinus taeda
Zones 6–9

Our most important and widely cultivated timber species in the southern United States

Are the needles mostly 3–6" (7.6–15.2 cm) long?

OR

Are the needles mostly ¾–4" (1.9–10.2 cm) long?

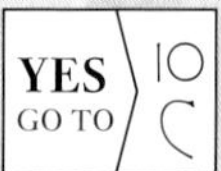

Are the needles 4–6" (10.2–15.2 cm) long, flexible, but break cleanly when folded; the bud and bark of the trunk reddish-brown? It is a **red pine.**

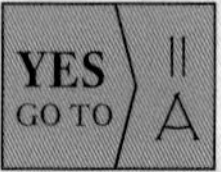

OR

Are the needles 3–6" (7.6–15.2 cm) long, stout and stiff; the bark of the trunk gray-brown with black furrows and the bud silvery? It is an **Austrian pine.**

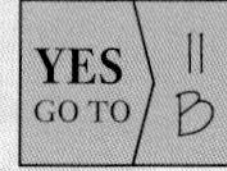

Are the needles mostly ¾–1½" (1.9–3.8 cm) long, yellow-green, and widely spread in bunches? **CLUE:** *The cones often remain closed for many years.* It is a **jack pine (scrub pine).**

OR

Are the needles 1½–4" (3.8–10.2 cm) long, blue-green to yellow-green, and twisted; and is the bark on the upper trunk of older trees orange-red? It is a **Scots pine.**

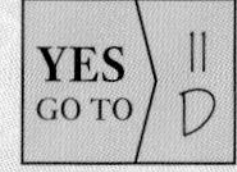

Are the needles 5–10" (12.7–25.4 cm) long, cones 3–6" (7.6–15.2 cm) long? **CLUE:** *The tree is native to the Great Plains and the West.* It is a **ponderosa pine.**

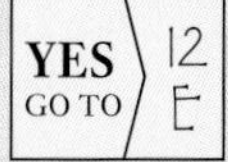

OR

Are the needles 7–10" (17.8–25.4 cm) long, cones 3–6" (7.6–15.2 cm) long? **CLUE:** *The tree is native to the southeastern states, especially along the coastal plain.* It is a **slash pine.**

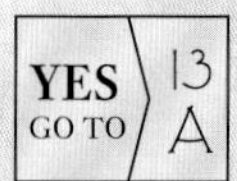

OR

Are the needles 3–5" (7.6–12.7 cm) long, cones 1½–2½" (3.8–6.4 cm) long? **CLUE:** *The tree is native to the southern states and north to central Missouri across to Pennsylvania.* It is a **shortleaf pine.**

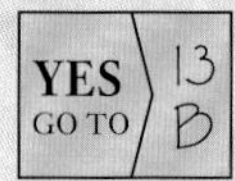

11A RED PINE, NORWAY PINE

Pinus resinosa
Zones 2–5

For telephone poles, lumber or wind-breaks, red pine is one 'hard-working tree'

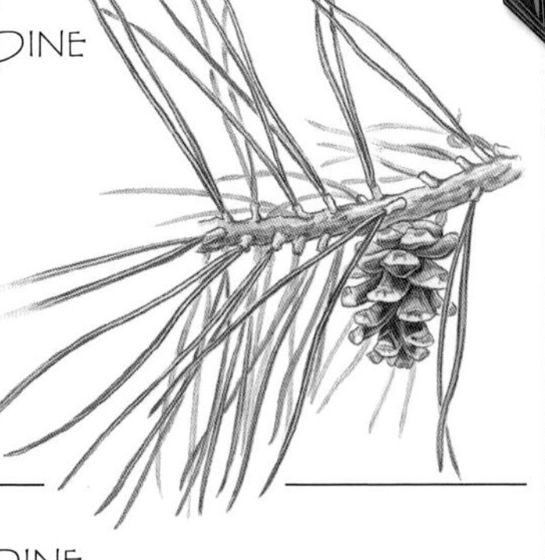

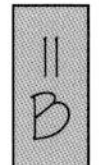

11B AUSTRIAN PINE

Pinus nigra
Zones 4–7

From southern Europe and Asia minor to wide-spread planting in our country on sites where only the drought-tolerant can thrive

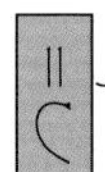

11C JACK PINE, SCRUB PINE

Pinus banksiana
Zones 2–7

An essential link for nesting cover in the precarious life cycle of the beautiful Kirtland's warbler

11D SCOTS PINE

Pinus sylvestris
Zones 3–7

Look for the orange bark atop this tree

12A

Are the cones less than ¾" (1.9 cm) long, with few scales; and are the small branches stiff and not drooping? It is a **tamarack (eastern larch).**

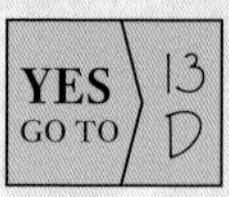

OR

Are the cones greater than ¾" (1.9 cm) long, with many scales; and do the small branches hang down? It is a **European larch.**

YES GO TO 13D

12B

Are the needles fairly easy to roll between your fingers? **CLUE:** *Needles are 4-sided or diamond-shaped in cross section.* These are spruce trees.

YES GO TO 14A

OR

Are the needles difficult to roll between your fingers? **CLUE:** *Needles are fairly flat in cross section.*

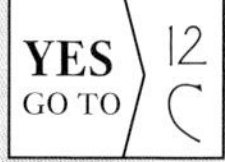

12C

Do the needles have 2 white or silvery stripes on their undersides?

YES GO TO 12D

OR

Are the needles green on both sides and flattened along the twigs, the cone a 1" diameter wrinkled ball? The needles and fine twigs are DECIDUOUS. It is a **baldcypress.**

YES GO TO 14D

12D

Do the cones hang down?

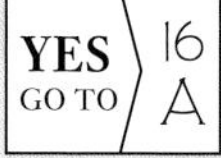

OR

Are the cones upright on top branches, over 1½" (3.8 cm) long with DECIDUOUS scales, the twigs fairly smooth where needles have fallen off? **CLUE:** *The bark is smooth for many years with resin blisters.* It is a **balsam fir or Fraser fir.**

YES GO TO 15A

13 A — Slash Pine

Pinus elliottii
Zones 8–10

Fast growth and useful wood make this a popular plantation tree in the South

13 B — Shortleaf Pine

Pinus echinata
Zones 6–9

Its prickly cones are like 'hedgehogs,' but its good wood and wide distribution earn it a place of respect in the southern timber industry

13 C — Tamarack, Eastern Larch

Larix laricina
Zones 2–5

This conifer drops its needles each fall and welcomes spring with fresh green growth

13 D — European Larch

Larix decidua
Zones 3–6

As yellowing needles drop each autumn, a golden carpet spreads beneath the tree

Are the mature cones generally over 2" (5.1 cm) long, with cone scale edges wavy or wedge-shaped?

YES GO TO 14 B

OR

Are the mature cones generally under 2" (5.1 cm) long, with cone scale edges rounded?

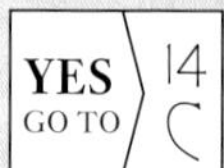

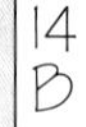

Are the needles not prickly-tipped, the cones 4–8" (10.2–20.3 cm) long, the branches drooping up to several feet on older trees? It is a **Norway spruce.**

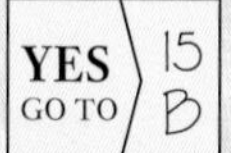

OR

Are the needle tips very sharp-pointed, cones 2–4" (5.1–10.2 cm) long, and the branches do not droop? It is a **Colorado blue spruce.**

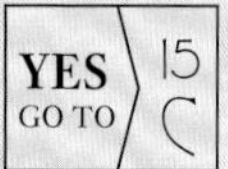

Are the needles ¼–½" (0.6–1.3 cm) long, dull blue-green; twigs with fine hairs; cones about 1" (2.5 cm) long and remaining on the tree for several years? It is a **black spruce.**

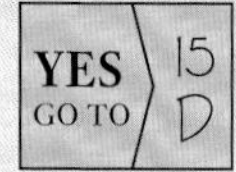

OR

Are the needles about ½" (1.3 cm) long, dark yellow-green and shiny; twigs with fine hairs; cones 1¼–2" (3.2–5.1 cm) and shed annually? It is a **red spruce.**

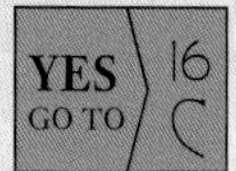

OR

Are the needles about ½" (1.3 cm) long, blue-green to silvery-white; twigs hairless; cones 1–2½" (2.5–6.4 cm) long with flexible scales, cones shed annually? It is a **white spruce.**

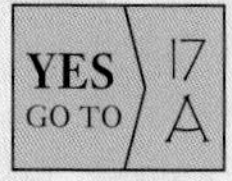

15A BALSAM FIR | FRASER FIR

Abies balsamea
Zones 3–6

Abies fraseri
Zones 4–7

The classic Christmas tree – most popular in both our nations

NOTE: Balsam fir is native to the northeastern U.S. and Canada, while Fraser fir is native to VA, NC, and TN.

15B NORWAY SPRUCE

Picea abies
Zones 3–7

Sometimes they stand as lone sentinels at ghostly farm sites where settlers once brought this reminder of the Old Country

15C COLORADO BLUE SPRUCE

Picea pungens
Zones 2–8

A favorite for striking contrast in lawns and border plantings

15D BLACK SPRUCE

Picea mariana
Zones 3–6

Found from Alaska, through Canada to Rhode Island, this is a spruce of swampy places with dark needles

Are the twigs rough where needles have fallen off, and the cones less than 1" (2.5 cm) long? It is an **eastern hemlock.**

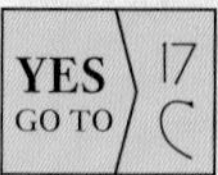

OR

Are the needles of equal length, the cones 3–4" (7.6–10.2 cm) long with a three-pointed BRACT sticking out of each scale? It is a **Douglasfir.**

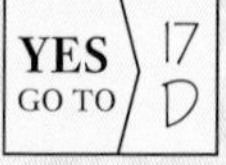

16
B

Are the leaves yellow-green, flattened and scale-like on outer twigs, foliage arranged in flat, fan-like sprays; fruit a small, bell-shaped, woody cone? It is an **eastern arborvitae (northern whitecedar).**

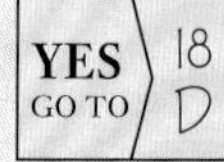

OR

Are the leaves dark blue-green, the foliage not arranged in flattened sprays; fruit a small brownish-purple, berry-like cone? It is an **Atlantic whitecedar (southern whitecedar).**

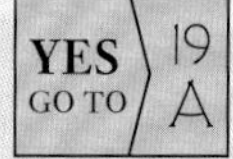

OR

Are the leaves dark green, blue-green, or purple-green, awl-shaped and scale-like on the same plant, foliage not arranged in flattened sprays; fruit is blue and berry-like? It is an **eastern redcedar.**

17A

WHITE SPRUCE

Picea glauca
Zones 2–6

Widespread through northern forests, but not where fires occur frequently. The reason: seeds are not produced until about age 30

17B

EASTERN HEMLOCK, CANADA HEMLOCK

Tsuga canadensis
Zones 3–8

Tiny needles and tiny cones adorn this tree in the cool, moist glens of eastern forests

17C

DOUGLASFIR

Pseudotsuga menziesii
Zones 4–6

See the 'mouse' scurry for cover between the cone scales!

17D

EASTERN ARBORVITAE, NORTHERN WHITECEDAR

Thuja occidentalis
Zones 3–7

A favorite for dense, beautiful living fences

18 A

Do the leaves have 3–5 LOBES (projections) in PALMATE arrangement (like fingers on a hand)? These are maple trees.

OR

Do the leaves look heart-shaped with a long, tapering tip and smooth outer edges and BLADES (the flat part of a leaf) that are 8–15" (20.3–38.1 cm) long? **CLUE:** *The fruit is a thin, brown seed pod 8–20" (20.3–50.8 cm) long.* It is a **northern catalpa.**

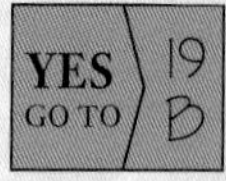

OR

Are the leaves ENTIRE (smooth, UN-TOOTHED edges), BLADES less than 8" (20.3 cm) long, with veins that curve to follow the leaf edge? It is a **flowering dogwood.**

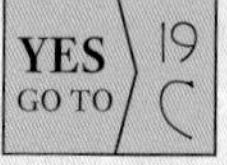

---

18 B

Do the leaves have closely TOOTHED edges with sharp V-shaped SINUS-ES (indentations)? **CLUE:** *The leaf underside is often silvery-white.*

OR

Do the leaves have smooth edges, or few TEETH (notches on the outer edge of a leaf) with rounded SINUSES?

YES GO TO 20 B

---

18 C

Do the flowers appear with or after the leaves in spring, the SAMARAS (winged fruits) maturing in late summer; leaves are 3-LOBED and sharply TOOTHED; bark marked by vertical, broad, white stripes? It is a **striped maple.**

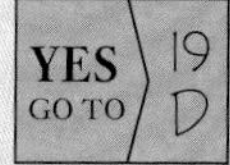

SAMARA

OR

Do the flowers appear before the leaves in spring, and the SAMARAS mature and drop in late spring; with bark not as above?

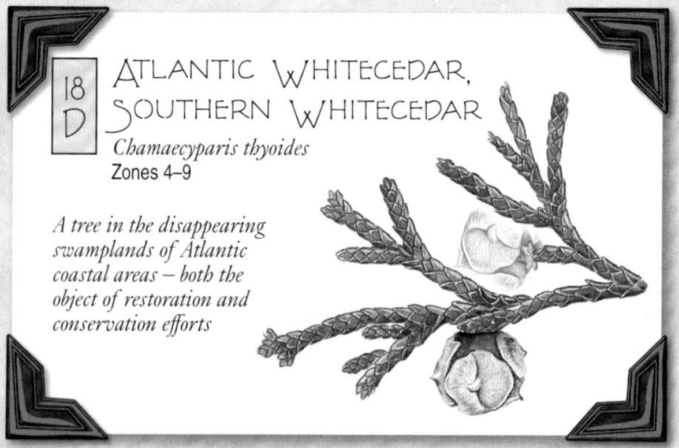

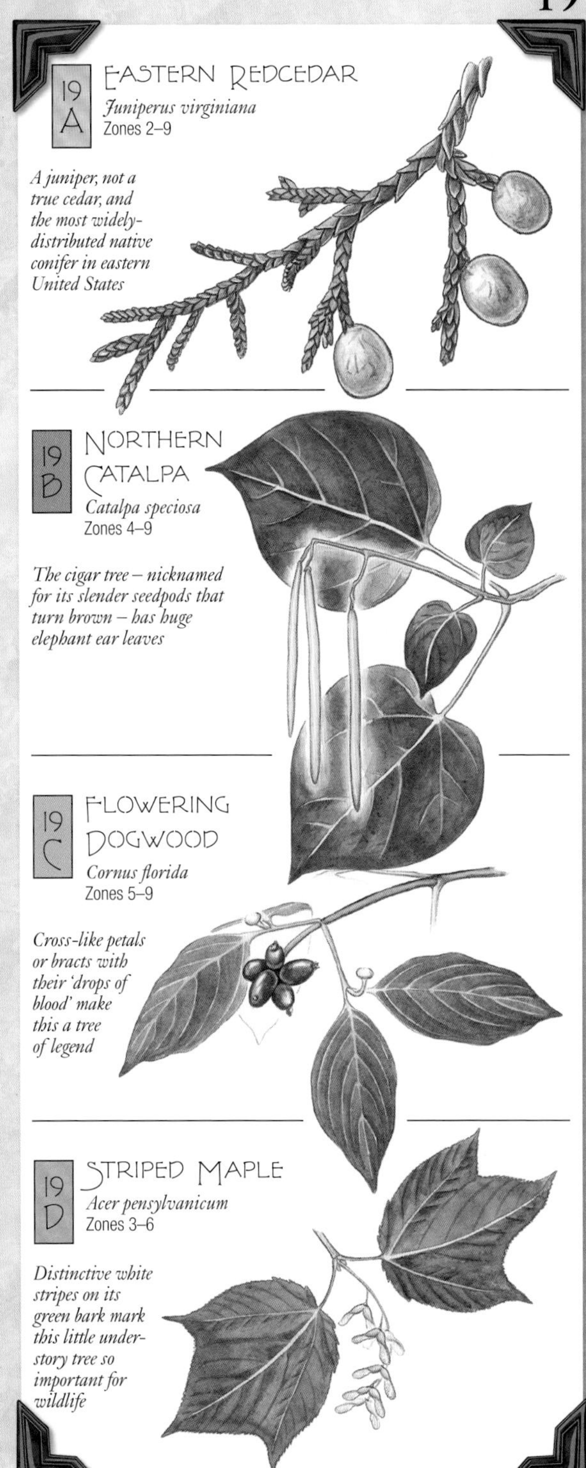

19A EASTERN REDCEDAR

Juniperus virginiana
Zones 2–9

A juniper, not a true cedar, and the most widely-distributed native conifer in eastern United States

19B NORTHERN CATALPA

Catalpa speciosa
Zones 4–9

The cigar tree – nicknamed for its slender seedpods that turn brown – has huge elephant ear leaves

19C FLOWERING DOGWOOD

Cornus florida
Zones 5–9

Cross-like petals or bracts with their 'drops of blood' make this a tree of legend

19D STRIPED MAPLE

Acer pensylvanicum
Zones 3–6

Distinctive white stripes on its green bark mark this little under-story tree so important for wildlife

20

Are the leaves about 4" (10.2 cm) across, mostly 3-LOBED (some 5); the SAMARA about ¾" (1.9 cm) long? It is a **red maple.**

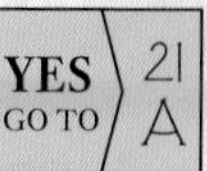

OR

Are the leaves about 6" (15.2 cm) across, deeply 5-LOBED; the SAMARA about 2" (5.1 cm) long? It is a **silver maple.**

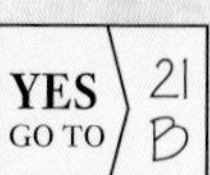

Do PETIOLES (the leaf stalk that connects the BLADE to the twig) not show milky sap when broken; buds are brown to dark brown, slender and pointed; the leaf underside is DOWNY or paler than the top?

OR

Do PETIOLES show milky sap when broken (may not show if very dry or in autumn); buds are green or red, stout and blunt; the leaf underside is not DOWNY or paler than the top? It is a **Norway maple.**

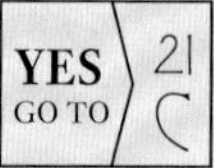

Are the leaves mostly 5-LOBED and usually not DOWNY on the underside, with red-brown twigs? It is a **sugar maple.**

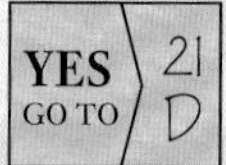

OR

Are the leaves mostly 3-LOBED, drooping, and DOWNY on the underside, with orange-brown twigs? It is a **black maple.**

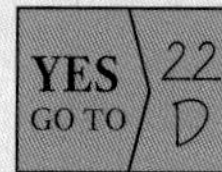

Are the leaves PALMATELY COMPOUND (BLADES arranged like fingers on a hand)? **CLUE:** *The fruit is a 3-part leathery CAPSULE with smooth, hard, nut-like seeds inside.*

PALMATE

OR

Are the leaves PINNATELY COMPOUND (BLADES arranged like the vanes of a feather)? **CLUE:** *The fruit is a single or double SAMARA.*

PINNATE

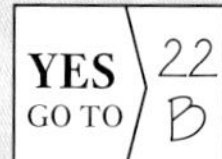

Are there usually 7 BLADES (the flat part of a leaf or leaflet, characteristic of BROADLEAF trees) with the buds normally gummy? It is a **horsechestnut.**

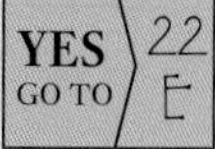

OR

Are there usually 5 BLADES with the buds not normally gummy?

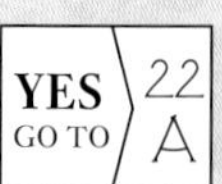

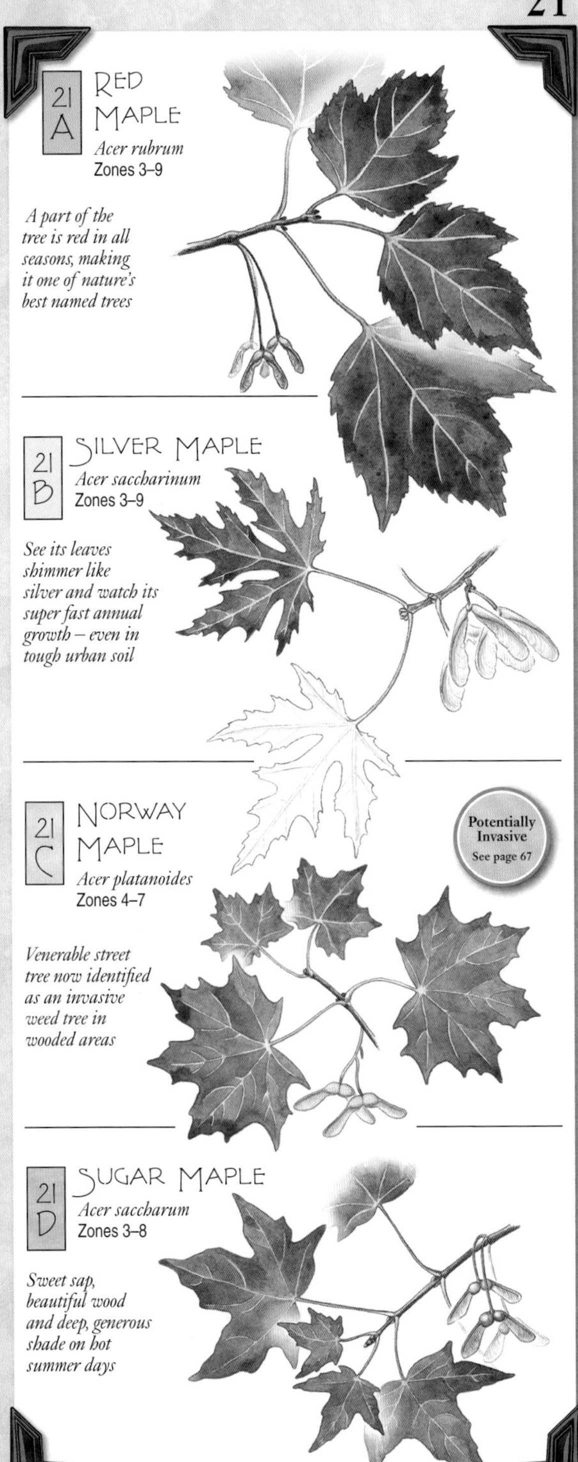

21 A RED MAPLE

Acer rubrum
Zones 3–9

A part of the tree is red in all seasons, making it one of nature's best named trees

21 B SILVER MAPLE

Acer saccharinum
Zones 3–9

See its leaves shimmer like silver and watch its super fast annual growth – even in tough urban soil

21 C NORWAY MAPLE

Acer platanoides
Zones 4–7

Potentially Invasive
See page 67

Venerable street tree now identified as an invasive weed tree in wooded areas

21 D SUGAR MAPLE

Acer saccharum
Zones 3–8

Sweet sap, beautiful wood and deep, generous shade on hot summer days

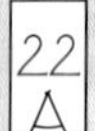

22A Do crushed twigs have a strong, unpleasant odor? **CLUE:** *The outside of the fruit is prickly.* It is an **Ohio Buckeye.** — **YES** GO TO 23A

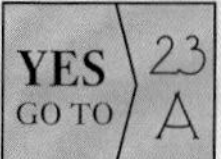

OR

Do crushed twigs not have a strong, unpleasant odor? **CLUE:** *The outside of the fruit is not prickly.* It is a **yellow buckeye.** — **YES** GO TO 23B

22B Are there mostly 3–5 BLADES that are LOBED or coarsely TOOTHED, with twigs green to purplish-green? **CLUE:** *The fruit is a double SAMARA.* It is a **boxelder (ashleaf maple).** — **YES** GO TO 23C

SAMARA

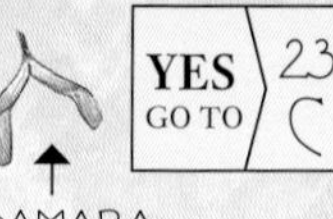

OR

Are there mostly 5–13 BLADES with smooth or TOOTHED edges? **CLUE:** *The fruit is a single SAMARA.* These are ash trees. — **YES** GO TO 22C

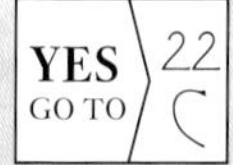

22C Are the young twigs rounded? — **YES** GO TO 24A

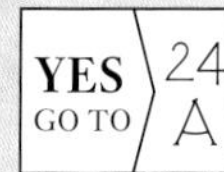

OR

Are the young twigs four sided or squarish? It is a **blue ash.** — **YES** GO TO 23D

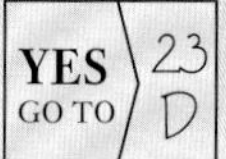

22D BLACK MAPLE

Acer nigrum

Zones 4–8

A close cousin of sugar maple but with a darker complexion when older

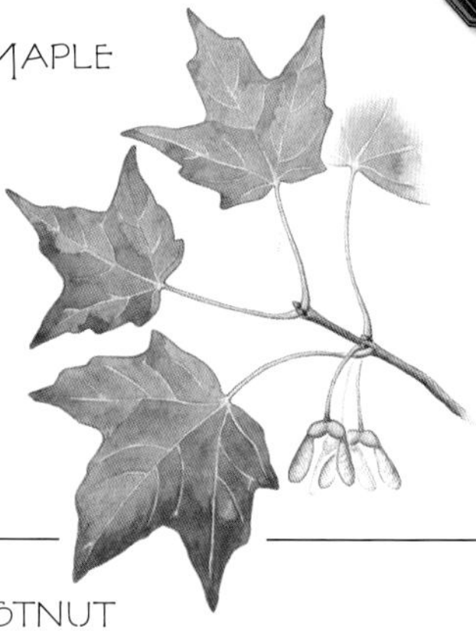

22E HORSECHESTNUT

Aesculus hippocastanum

Zones 4–7

Large white flowers held aloft like torches in the spring yield shiny buckeyes by fall

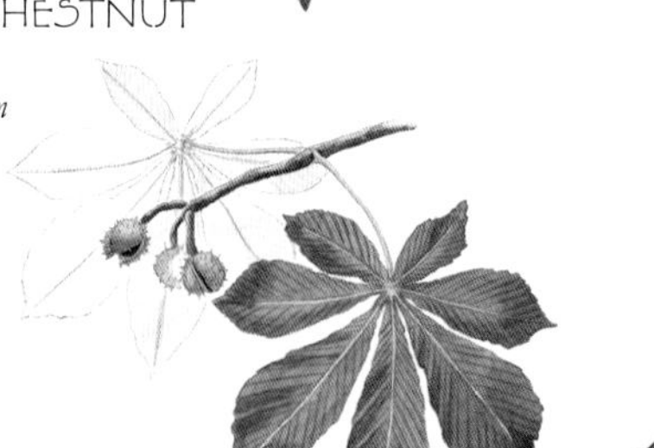

23 A OHIO BUCKEYE

Aesculus glabra
Zones 4–7

See what early Native Americans called the "eye of a buck" in the fruit of this enjoyable tree

23 B YELLOW BUCKEYE

Aesculus flava (octandra)
Zones 4–8

Largest of the buckeye trees

23 C BOXELDER, ASHLEAF MAPLE

Acer negundo
Zones 3–9

Another and probably better name for boxelder, this maple is the only one with compound leaves

23 D BLUE ASH

Fraxinus quadrangulata
Zones 4–7

Nature's oddity with 4-sided twigs!

24A Are the LEAF SCARS (the mark left where the leaf was previously attached) nearly straight across the top; leaves with yellow fall color? It is a **green ash.**

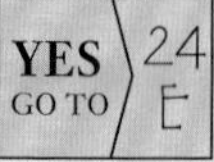

YES GO TO 24E

OR

Are the LEAF SCARS deeply notched at the top or U-shaped; leaf underside often whitish, leaves with a bronze to purple fall color? It is a **white ash.**

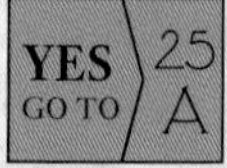

YES GO TO 25A

24B Are the leaves fan-shaped, the veins fanning out from the leaf base, with 1 or 2 notches forming LOBES along the MARGIN (the edge of a leaf), and most attached to short, SPUR-like branches? It is a CONIFER known as **gingko.**

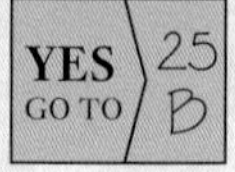

YES GO TO 25B

OR

Are the leaves not fan-shaped?

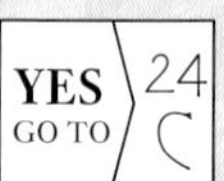

YES GO TO 24C

24C Are the leaves flattened across the top, with 2 LOBES on either side of the MIDRIB (the primary rib or central vein)? It is a **yellow-poplar, tulip-poplar, tuliptree.**

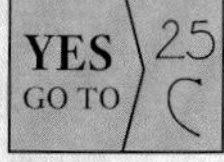

YES GO TO 25C

OR

Are the leaves ENTIRE, mitten-shaped, or 3-LOBED all on the same small tree or shrub? It is a **sassafras.**

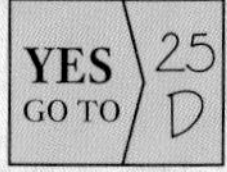

YES GO TO 25D

OR

Are the leaves TOOTHED, LOBED and UNLOBED on the same tree, the fruit fleshy?

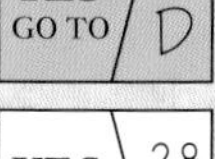

YES GO TO 28E

OR

Are the leaves and fruit not as above?

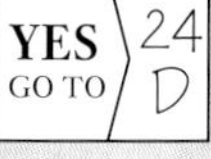

YES GO TO 24D

24D Are most of the leaves LOBED (sometimes LOBED and non-LOBED leaves appear on the same tree)?

YES GO TO 26A

OR

Are the leaves not LOBED?

YES GO TO 34C

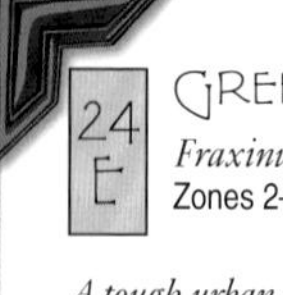

24E GREEN ASH

Fraxinus pennsylvanica

Zones 2–9

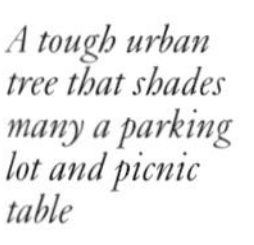

A tough urban tree that shades many a parking lot and picnic table

25 A

White Ash

Fraxinus americana
Zones 3–9

The wood giving us the 'crack of the bat' at baseball games

25 B

Ginkgo

Ginkgo biloba
Zones 4–8

A living fossil – leaves are found imprinted in rocks from the days of dinosaurs

25 C

Yellow-Poplar, Tulip-Poplar, Tuliptree

Liriodendron tulipifera
Zones 4–9

"Imagine a tall tree with unearthly foliage and 5,000 tulips in its hair."

—Thomas Pakenham in Meetings With Remarkable Trees

25 D

Sassafras

Sassafras albidum
Zones 4–9

Three shapes of leaves on each tree and the sweetest tea offered by nature

Are the leaves, when LOBED, irregularly or distinctly PINNATELY (like the vanes of a feather) LOBED ?

OR

Are the leaves, when LOBED, PALMATELY (like fingers on the palm of a hand) LOBED?

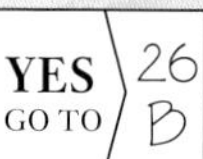

OR

Are the leaves slightly LOBED or non-LOBED, rounded, variable in size and shape and 1–4" (2.5–10.2 cm) long? **CLUE:** *The fruit is an acorn.* It is a **water oak.**

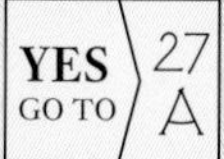

Are the leaves star-shaped, with 5–7 LOBES and finely-TOOTHED MARGINS? **CLUE:** *The fruit is a spiked ball.* It is a **sweetgum.**

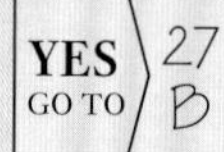

OR

Are the leaves not star-shaped, with 3–5 LOBES?

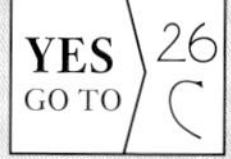

Are the leaves at least 4–10" (10.2–25.4 cm) wide, the PETIOLE base hollow, covering the side buds; the bark of the upper trunk and branches smooth or peeling off in large sections? **CLUE:** *The fruit is a dry ball on a long stalk.*

OR

Are the leaves 1–4" (2.5–10.2 cm) wide, some not LOBED, with undersides and twigs covered with white hair, the base of the PETIOLE not hollow or covering the side buds? It is a **white poplar.**

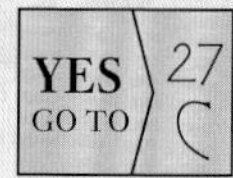

Do most of the seed balls grow singly? It is an **American sycamore.**

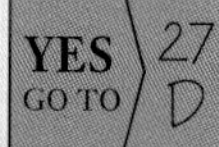

OR

Do most of the seed balls grow in pairs? It is a **London planetree.**

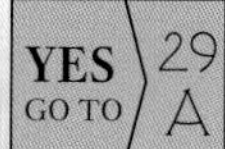

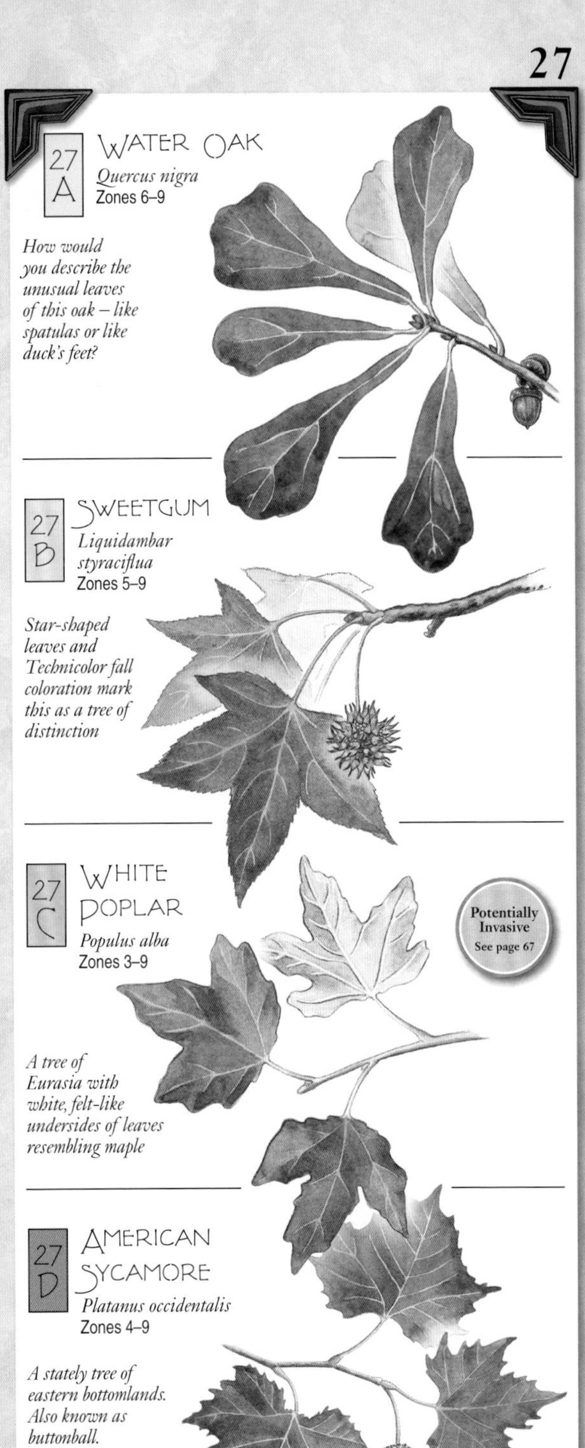
27
A
WATER OAK
Quercus nigra
Zones 6–9
How would you describe the unusual leaves of this oak – like spatulas or like duck's feet?
27
B
SWEETGUM
Liquidambar styraciflua
Zones 5–9
Star-shaped leaves and Technicolor fall coloration mark this as a tree of distinction
27
C
WHITE POPLAR
Populus alba
Zones 3–9
Potentially Invasive
See page 67
A tree of Eurasia with white, felt-like undersides of leaves resembling maple
27
D
AMERICAN SYCAMORE
Platanus occidentalis
Zones 4–9
A stately tree of eastern bottomlands. Also known as buttonball.

Do the twigs have slender, tapered thorns? These are hawthorn trees.

OR

Do the twigs not have slender, tapered thorns?

Are the leaves generally LOBED and smooth? **CLUE:** *The red fruit or POME is ¼" (.6 cm) in diameter, ripening in early fall.* It is a **Washington hawthorn.**

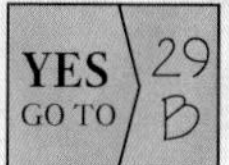

OR

Are the leaves generally LOBED and DOWNY? **CLUE:** *The red fruit (POME) is ½–1" (1.3–2.5 cm) in diameter, ripening in late summer.* It is a **downy hawthorn.**

Are the leaves DOWNY and jagged TOOTHED or slightly LOBED, the branches with short, stubby, sharp SPURS (twigs)? **CLUE:** *The fruit is a small apple.* It is a **prairie crabapple.**

OR

Are the leaves, twigs, and fruit not as above?

Do the leaves have 3 main veins coming out of the leaf base, several leaf shapes, one bud at the tip of each twig? **CLUE:** *The fruit is fleshy.* These are mulberry trees.

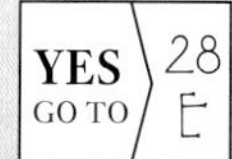

OR

Do the leaves have 1 large MIDRIB, with several buds clustered at the tip of each twig? **CLUE:** *The fruits are acorns.* These are oak trees.

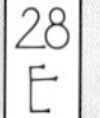

Are the leaves rough on top, UNLOBED to 3-LOBED; young twigs DOWNY, with fruit (on female trees) red to dark purple? It is a **red mulberry.**

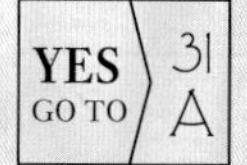

OR

Are the leaves smooth and glossy on top, UNLOBED to many-LOBED; young twigs not DOWNY, with fruit (on female trees) white, pink or purple? It is a **white mulberry.**

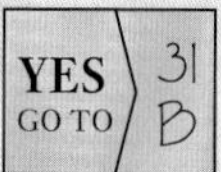

29 A — LONDON PLANETREE

Platanus x acerifolia
Zones 5–9

Attractive bark and roots tolerant to urban conditions make this a popular street and park tree

29 B — WASHINGTON HAWTHORN

Crataegus phaenopyrum
Zones 4–8

Showy white flowers blanket the crown in late spring

29 C — DOWNY HAWTHORN

Crataegus mollis
Zones 3–6

Omaha Indians once steeped the twigs of this tree to make tea

29 D — PRAIRIE CRABAPPLE

Malus ioensis
Zones 4–7

Fruits that are hard and sour, but with flowers showy and fragrant

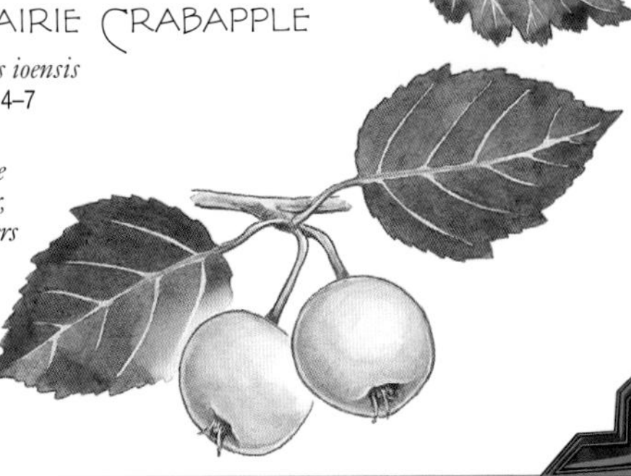

Are the LOBES blunt or rounded, not bristle tipped? **CLUE:** *The inner surface of the acorn shell, next to the fleshy acorn meat, is not DOWNY.*

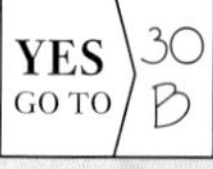

OR

Are the LOBES sharp and bristle tipped? **CLUE:** *The inner surface of the acorn shell is DOWNY.*

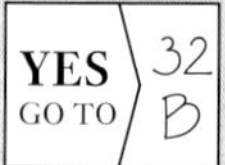

Are the leaves usually cross-shaped, with a very rough, sandpaper-like top surface? It is a **post oak.**

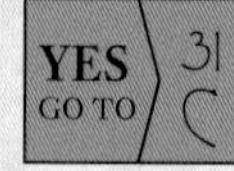

OR

Are the leaves not cross-shaped?

Are the leaves DOWNY on the underside? **CLUE:** *The edge of the acorn cap is unfringed to highly fringed and covers one third or more of the acorn.*

OR

Are the leaves smooth, not DOWNY, on the underside? **CLUE:** *The edge of the acorn cap is not fringed and covers one third or less of the acorn.*

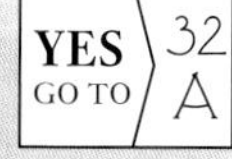

Does a bristly acorn cap enclose ½ or more of the acorn, with little or no stalk; leaves narrower toward the twig end, shallowly to deeply LOBED, often with a pair of deep SINUSES just below the leaf middle? **CLUE:** *The bark on twigs is often in corky ridges.* It is a **bur oak.**

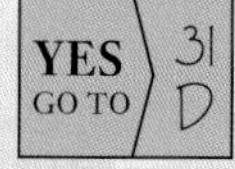

OR

Does a slightly fringed acorn cap enclose ½ or less of the acorn with the acorn on a 1–3" (2.5–7.6 cm) stalk; the leaves shallowly LOBED or with coarse rounded TEETH? **CLUE:** *The bark peels on upper branches and twigs.* It is a **swamp white oak.**

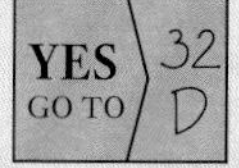

OR

Does the acorn cap nearly enclose the acorn, with the acorn stalk ½–1" (1.3–2.5 cm) long? It is an **overcup oak.**

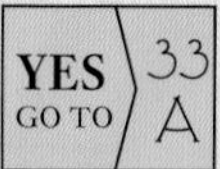

31 A

Red Mulberry

Morus rubra
Zones 5–9

Our native mulberry and highly popular with people and wildlife for its blackberry-like fruit

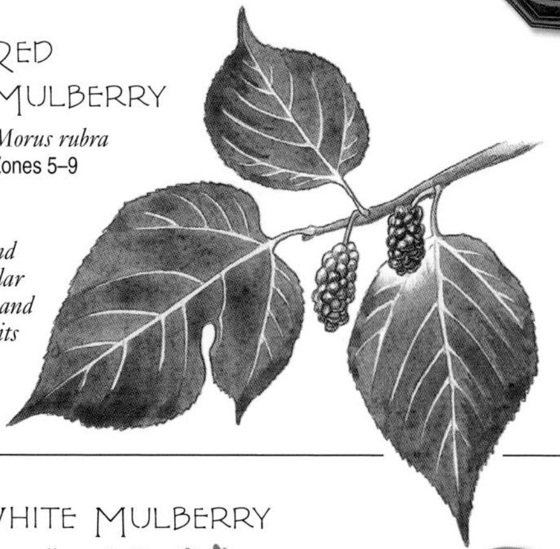

31 B

White Mulberry

Morus alba
Zones 4–9

Potentially Invasive
See page 67

A native of China, introduced here for silkworm culture in Colonial times

31 C

Post Oak

Quercus stellata
Zones 5–9

Distinctive leaves shaped like a Maltese cross – and a good choice for dry planting sites

31 D

Bur Oak

Quercus macrocarpa
Zones 3–8

The largest acorn of all our native oaks

Are the leaves 4–9" (10.2–22.9 cm) long; with the PETIOLE ½ to 1" (1.3–2.5 cm) long? It is a **white oak.**

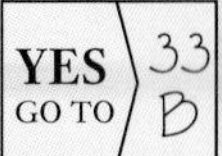

OR

Are the leaves 2–5" (5.1–12.7 cm) long with ear-lobe-like leaf bases and a very short or absent PETIOLE? It is an **English oak.**

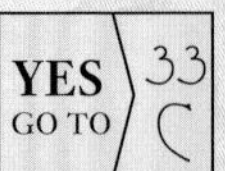

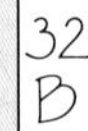

On the underside, are the leaves DOWNY with a gray to rust tint, with 3 shallow LOBED and 5–11 deep LOBED leaves on the same tree? **CLUE:** *The base of the leaves are U-shaped.* It is a **southern red oak.**

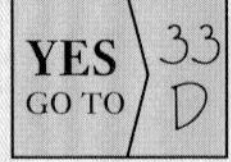

OR

Are the leaves not DOWNY or with just scattered tufts of hair along the veins on the underside?

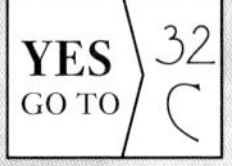

Are the leaves normally dull to slightly shiny on top with SINUSES that extend halfway or less to the MIDRIB? **CLUE:** *The acorns are ¾–1¼" (1.9–3.2 cm) long.* It is a **northern red oak.**

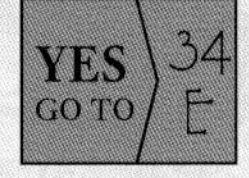

OR

Are the leaves normally shiny on the top with SINUSES that extend more than halfway to the MIDRIB? **CLUE:** *The acorns are ½–1" (1.3–2.5 cm) long.*

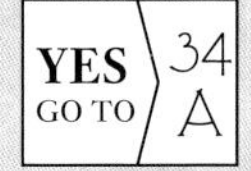

33 A OVERCUP OAK

Quercus lyrata
Zones 5–9

The oak of poorly drained flood plains and swamps of the southeast and a good choice for landscaping where water can be a problem

33 B WHITE OAK

Quercus alba
Zones 3–9

Our mighty oak, the most important species of the white oak group, is beautiful all year long

33 C ENGLISH OAK

Quercus robur
Zones 4–8

Robin Hood and Knights of Olde were familiar with this common native of Europe, western Asia and northern Africa

33 D SOUTHERN RED OAK

Quercus falcata
Zones 7–9

A fine street tree with leaves of various shapes but usually displaying very deep cuts between pointy lobes

Do the SINUSES extend about ⅔ of the way to the MIDRIB with a smooth upper leaf surface and sometimes hairy tufts and yellow to copper color on underside? It is a **black oak.**

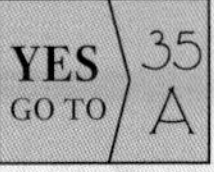

OR

Do the SINUSES extend more than ⅔ of the way to the MIDRIB?

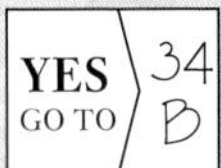

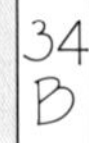

Does the acorn cap enclose ⅓–½ or more of the acorn? **CLUE:** The acorn often has several concentric rings (like a bullseye) around its tip. It is a **scarlet oak.**

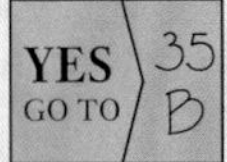

OR

Does the acorn cap only enclose the base of the acorn, with the acorn usually striped? It is a **pin oak.**

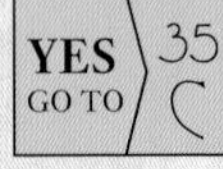

Are the leaf MARGINS ENTIRE?

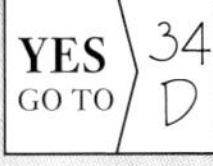

OR

Are the leaf MARGINS not ENTIRE?

Are the leaves, young twigs, and small, olive-like fruit covered with silvery scales, with thorns often present? It is a **Russian-olive.**

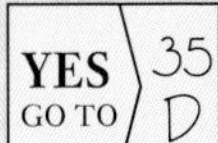

OR

Are the leaves, twigs, and fruit not covered with silvery scales?

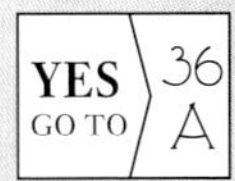

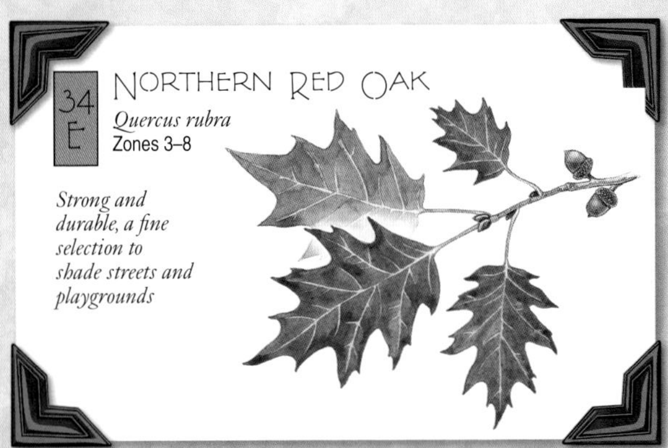

35A BLACK OAK

Quercus velutina
Zones 3–9

Yellow oak might be a better name for this tree with bright yellow or orange inner bark

35B SCARLET OAK

Quercus coccinea
Zones 4–9

Renowned for its relatively fast growth and brilliant scarlet color in autumn

35C PIN OAK

Quercus palustris
Zones 4–8

Its pyramid shape and single, central trunk make this a popular street and parking lot tree – but beware of planting in alkaline soil

35D RUSSIAN-OLIVE

Elaeagnus angustifolia
Zones 2–7

A culprit on the nation's Least Wanted list of invasive species

Potentially Invasive
See page 67

Are the leaves broad and heart-shaped and are the spring blooms purple? **CLUE:** *The fruit is a small pod or LEGUME.* It is an **eastern redbud.**

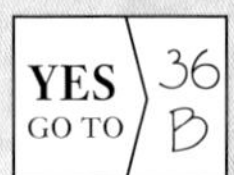

OR

Are the leaves not heart-shaped and the fruit not a pod?

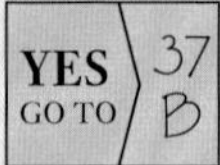

Do the twigs and leaves have milky sap, with spines or thorns often present on twigs? **CLUE:** *The fruit is large, green, and rough-textured.* It is an **Osage-orange.**

OR

Are the twigs and leaves without milky sap, the stems without spines, the fruit not as above?

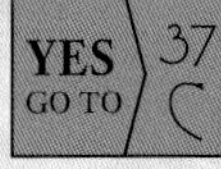

Are the leaves 6–12" (15.2–30.5 cm) long; the buds brown, naked or scaleless, covered with rusty hairs? **CLUE:** *The fruit is 2–5" (5.1–12.7 cm) long, fleshy, sweet, and brownish-black when ripe.* It is a **pawpaw.**

OR

Are the buds and fruit not as above?

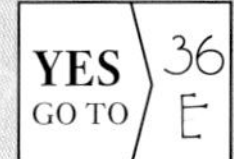

Are the leaves 3–24" (7.6–61 cm) long; twigs fairly smooth, encircled by thin SCARS or lines at each BUD; the flowers large and showy?

OR

Are the leaves smaller; twigs not encircled by thin SCARS or lines at each BUD, and the flowers not large and showy?

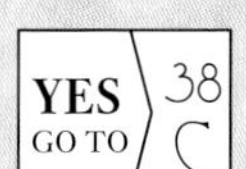

Are the leaves usually shorter than 10" (25.4 cm)?

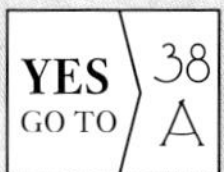

OR

Are the leaves 10–24" (25.4–61 cm) long, clustered near the ends of the branches giving an umbrella effect? **CLUE:** *The flowers are white and unpleasantly scented.* It is an **umbrella magnolia.**

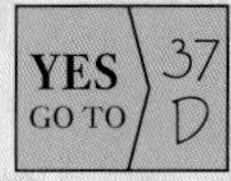

37 A — EASTERN REDBUD

Cercis canadensis
Zones 4–9

Pink blossoms spring from the bark and twigs— among the first in announcing the end of winter

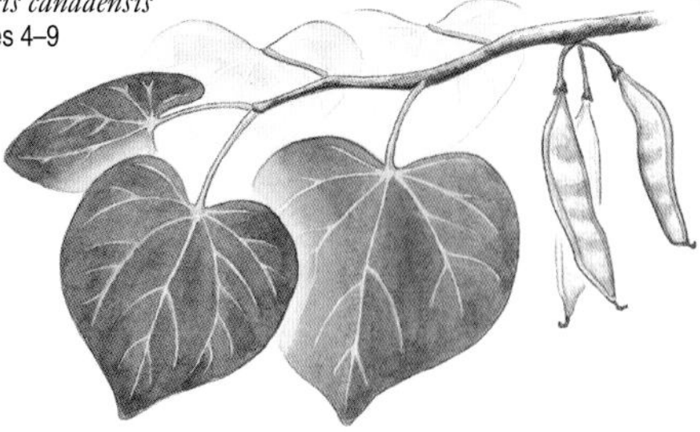

37 B — OSAGE-ORANGE

Maclura pomifera
Zones 4–9

Strange, grapefruit-sized fruits and wood that settlers found perfect for long-lasting fence posts

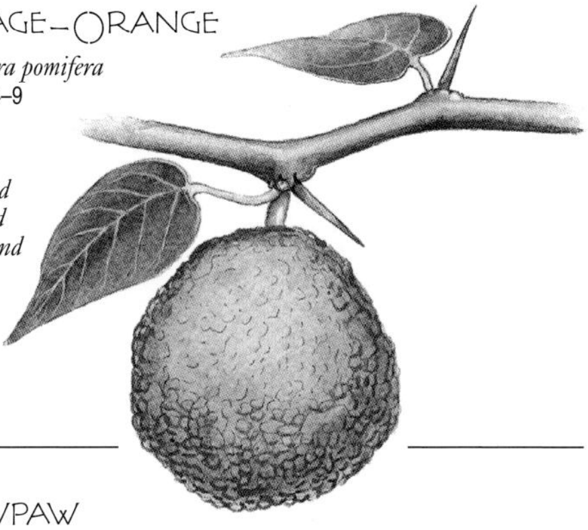

37 C — PAWPAW

Asimina triloba
Zones 5–8

"Pickin' up pawpaws and puttin' them in a basket" – and then eating these huge, custard-flavored fruits

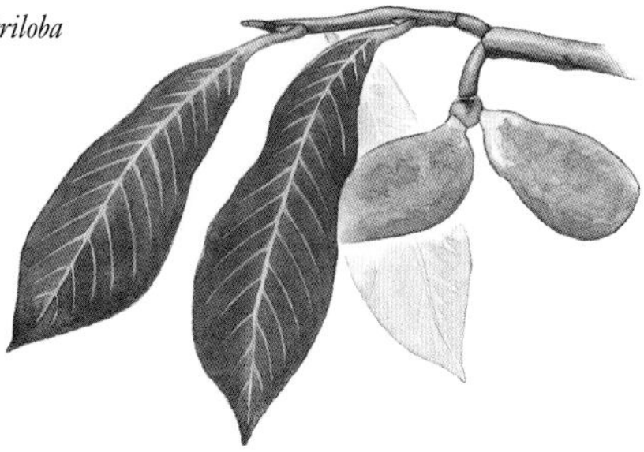

37 D — UMBRELLA MAGNOLIA

Magnolia tripetala
Zones 4–8

Super-sized leaves give a lush, tropical appearance to this little tree

Are the leaves EVERGREEN with rusty red hairs on the leaf underside and on the flower buds and twigs? **CLUE:** *The flowers are large, white, and pleasant smelling.* It is a **southern magnolia.**

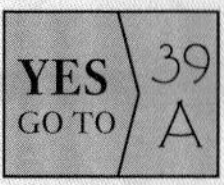

OR

Are the leaves not EVERGREEN, with their lower surfaces, twigs, and buds not covered with red hairs?

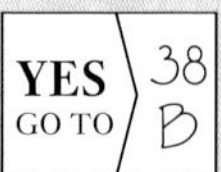

Are the leaves 3–6" (7.6–15.2 cm) long, the flowers large and white to pink to purple? It is a **saucer magnolia.**

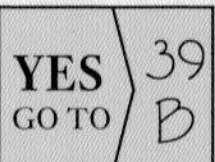

OR

Are the leaves 4–10" (10.2–25.4 cm) long, the flowers large and greenish-yellow? It is a **cucumbertree magnolia.**

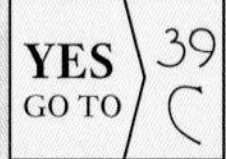

Are several buds clustered at the ends of the twigs, the leaves often tipped with a single bristle? **CLUE:** *The fruit is an acorn.*

OR

Are the buds not clustered at the ends of the twigs, the leaves not tipped with a bristle, and the fruit not an acorn?

Are the leaves thick, leathery, and EVERGREEN with an occasional TOOTHED leaf? It is a **live oak.**

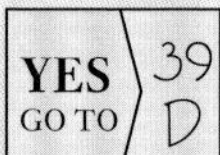

OR

Are the leaves not leathery and shed in the fall?

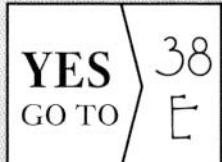

Are the leaves 2 or 3 times as long as wide, and DOWNY underneath? It is a **shingle oak.**

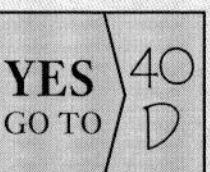

OR

Are the leaves very narrow and usually not DOWNY on the underside? It is a **willow oak.**

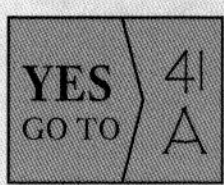

39 A
SOUTHERN MAGNOLIA
Magnolia grandiflora
Zones 6–10
Handsome and durable – an aristocrat of southern trees
39 B
SAUCER MAGNOLIA
Magnolia x soulangeana
Zones 5–9
Beautiful flowers open fully to present the 'saucer' in its name
39 C
CUCUMBERTREE MAGNOLIA
Magnolia acuminata
Zones 3–8
Look to the young knobby green fruits to see how this tree got its name
39 D
LIVE OAK
Quercus virginiana
Zones 7–10
With its mighty limbs spread wide and draped in Spanish moss, this is the classic tree of southern mansions and lawns

Is the fruit ½" (1.3 cm) long, blue-black, and berry-like? **CLUE:** *The PITH or center of the twigs is divided by woody plates.* It is a **black tupelo (blackgum).**

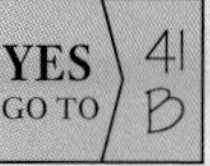

OR

Is the fruit an orange berry, 1–1½" (2.5–3.8 cm) in diameter? It is a **persimmon.**

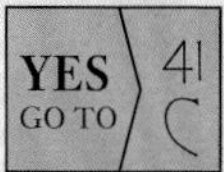

Are the leaves EVERGREEN, stiff, leathery, and tipped with hard pointy spines at the ends of the TEETH? **CLUE:** *The fruit is a red berry.* It is an **American holly.**

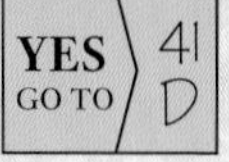

OR

Do the leaves not have hard, pointy spines?

Is the fruit a nut in a bur or an acorn in a cap?

YES GO TO 42 A

OR

Is the fruit not in a bur or cap?

YES GO TO 44 A

41 A WILLOW OAK

Quercus phellos
Zones 5–9

Leaves like a willow tree and easy to plant and grow

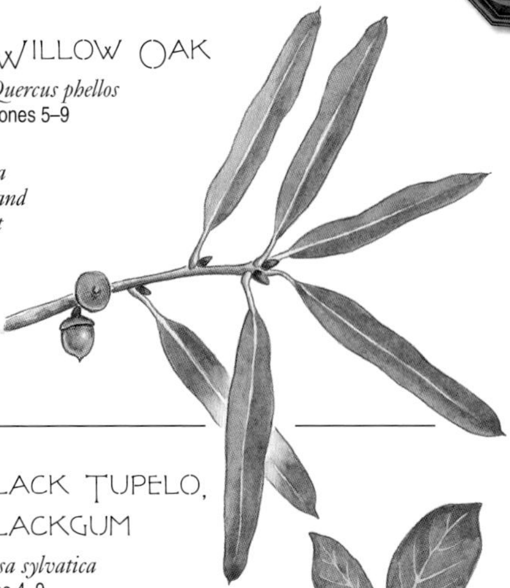

41 B BLACK TUPELO, BLACKGUM

Nyssa sylvatica
Zones 4–9

Flat, blocky bark on old trees and stunningly colorful fall foliage

41 C PERSIMMON

Diospyros virginiana
Zones 4–9

From bitter to sweet – be sure to wait for a hard frost before tasting its fruit

41 D AMERICAN HOLLY

Ilex opaca
Zones 5–9

A cheery symbol of the holiday season

42

Is there a single bud ⅛–¼" (0.125–0.6 cm) long at the end of each twig? **CLUE:** *The fruit is 2–3 rounded nuts in a prickly bur.* These are chestnut trees.

YES GO TO 42 B

OR

Are there several buds ⅛–¼" (0.125–0.6 cm) long at the end of each twig? **CLUE:** *The fruit is an acorn.* These are oak trees.

YES GO TO 42 C

OR

Are the buds ¾–1" (1.9–2.5 cm) long, with the fruit a bur enclosing 2–3 triangular nuts? **CLUE:** *The bark is thin and blue-gray.* It is an **American beech.**

Are the leaves yellow-green on top, with smooth undersides and twigs? It is an **American chestnut.**

YES GO TO 43 A

OR

Are the leaves reddish or dark green on top, with DOWNY undersides and twigs? It is a **Chinese chestnut.**

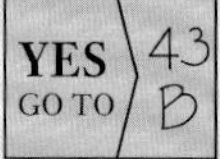

Do the leaves have large, rounded TEETH or short LOBES? **CLUE:** *The acorns have long (1–4", 2.5–10.2 cm) stalks.* It is a **swamp white oak.**

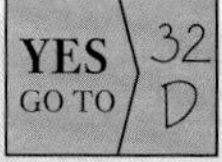

OR

Do the leaves have rounded TEETH? **CLUE:** *The acorns have a short stalk.* It is a **chestnut oak.**

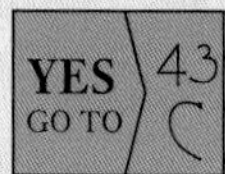

OR

Do the leaves have sharp TEETH? **CLUE:** *The acorns have almost no stalk.* It is a **chinkapin oak.**

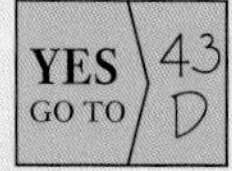

43A American Chestnut

Castanea dentata
Zones 4–8

Once mighty and proud, brought down by a blight that now strikes at the juveniles that continue to sprout from ancient roots

43B Chinese Chestnut

Castanea mollissima
Zones 4–8

After our native chestnut fell to the blight, this resident of China helped fill the void

43C Chestnut Oak

Quercus prinus
Zones 4–8

The likely oak found if you are hiking a rocky ridge top in the Appalachian Mountains

43D Chinkapin Oak

Quercus muehlenbergii
Zones 4–7

Humingbirds and butterflies are particularly fond of this fine oak tree

Do the branches have sharp SPUR twigs or thorns?

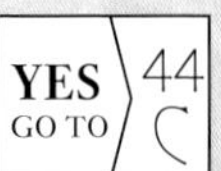

OR

Do the twigs and branches not have thorns?

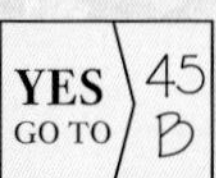

Is the fruit fleshy with a single, stony seed and about 1" (2.5 cm) in diameter when mature? It is an **American plum.**

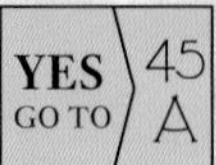

OR

Is the fruit fleshy, ½" (1.3 cm) or less in diameter when mature, with more than one seed? It is a **cockspur hawthorn.**

Do the leaves have flattened PETIOLES? These are aspen or cottonwood trees.

OR

Do the leaves not have flattened PETIOLES?

Are the leaves dark green on top, heart shaped to nearly round with rounded or slightly flattened bases, and abruptly pointed tips?

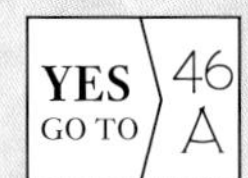

OR

Are the leaves bright green to yellow-green and generally triangular, with flat to rounded bases?

OR

Are the leaves dark green on top with rounded or heart shaped bases, twice as long as wide, with sharply pointed tips? **CLUE:** *Two-part seed CAPSULE that is not hairy.* It is a **balsam poplar.**

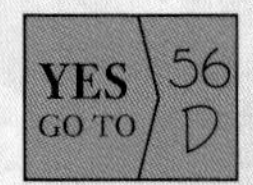

Are the leaf MARGINS finely TOOTHED? It is a **quaking aspen.**

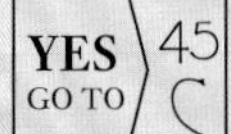

OR

Are the leaf MARGINS coarsely TOOTHED? It is a **bigtooth aspen.**

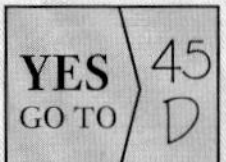

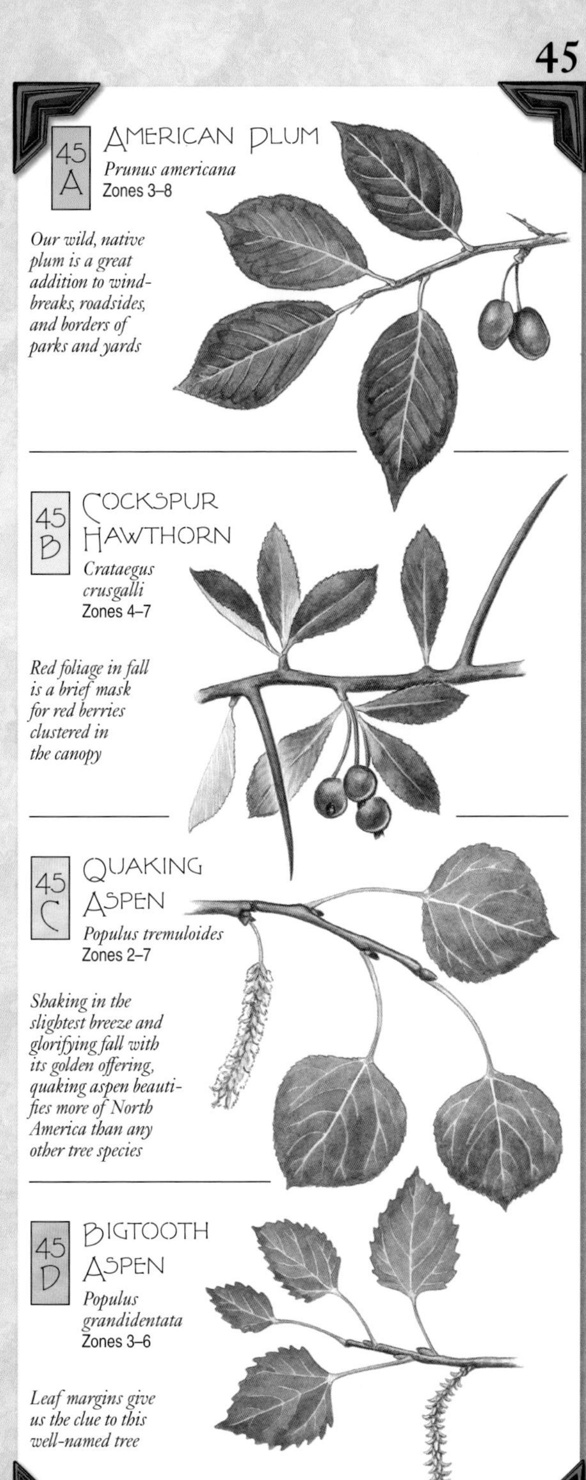

45 A AMERICAN PLUM

Prunus americana
Zones 3–8

Our wild, native plum is a great addition to windbreaks, roadsides, and borders of parks and yards

45 B COCKSPUR HAWTHORN

Crataegus crusgalli
Zones 4–7

Red foliage in fall is a brief mask for red berries clustered in the canopy

45 C QUAKING ASPEN

Populus tremuloides
Zones 2–7

Shaking in the slightest breeze and glorifying fall with its golden offering, quaking aspen beautifies more of North America than any other tree species

45 D BIGTOOTH ASPEN

Populus grandidentata
Zones 3–6

Leaf margins give us the clue to this well-named tree

Does this tree have a narrow, column shape with the branches reaching almost straight upward? It is a **Lombardy black poplar.**

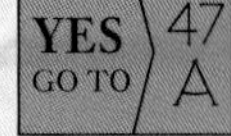

OR

Does the tree have more spreading shape? **CLUE:** *The leaves have 2 glands where the leaf BLADE meets the PETIOLE.*

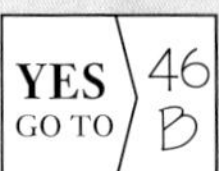

Are the leaf MARGINS finely TOOTHED and the buds smooth? It is an **eastern cottonwood.**

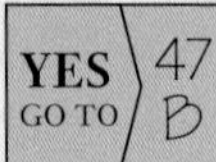

OR

Are the leaf MARGINS coarsely TOOTHED and the buds slightly DOWNY? **CLUE:** *This tree is native to the Great Plains and Rocky Mountains.* It is a **plains cottonwood.**

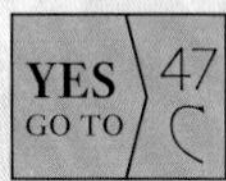

Do the leaves have 3–5 veins radiating from the base?

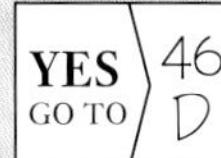

OR

Do the leaves have 1 MIDRIB?

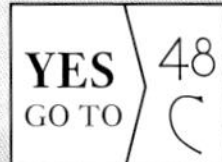

Is the sap milky, are some leaves LOBED with leaf bases similar on both sides of the PETIOLE? **CLUE:** *The fruit is fleshy and bumpy.* These are mulberry trees.

OR

Is the sap not milky, the leaf bases different on both sides of the PETIOLE? **CLUE:** *The fruit has a single hard seed.*

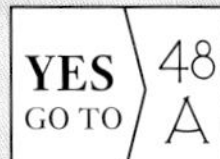

Are the leaves rough on top; young twigs DOWNY, with fruit (on female trees) red to dark purple? It is a **red mulberry.**

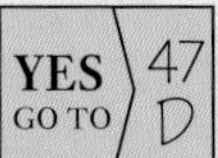

OR

Are the leaves smooth and glossy on top; young twigs not DOWNY, with fruit (on female trees) white, pink or purple? It is a **white mulberry.**

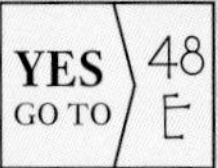

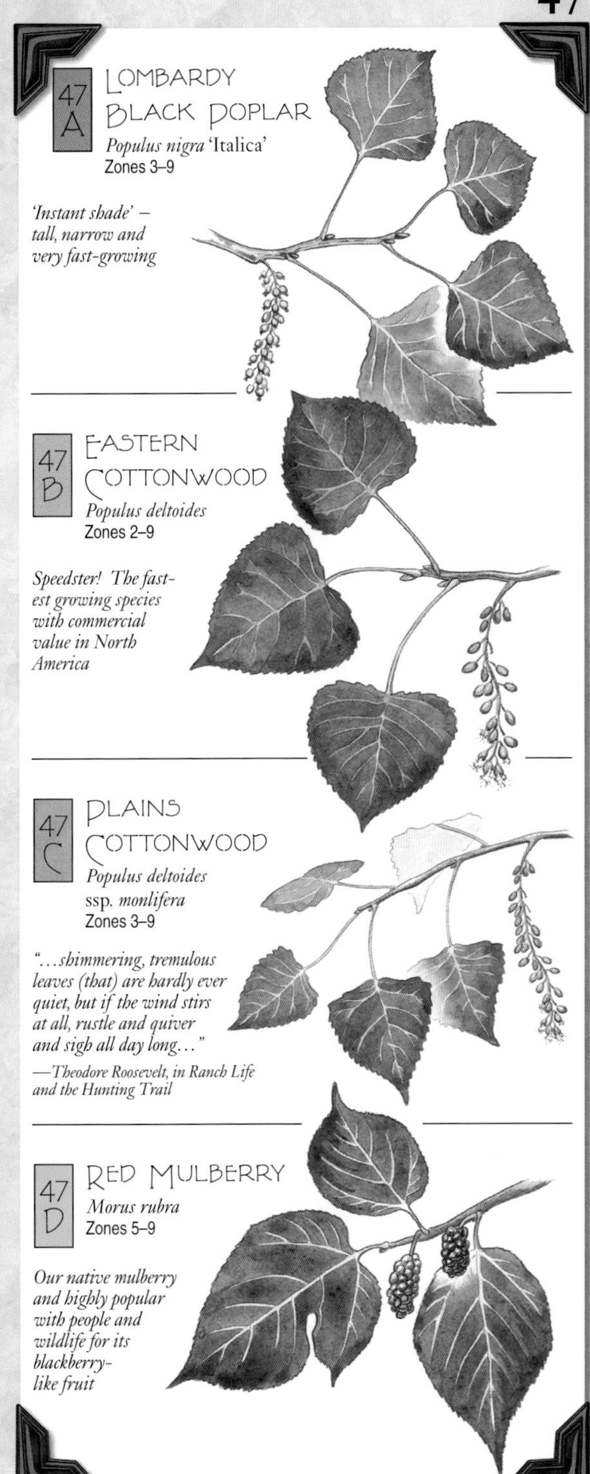

47A LOMBARDY BLACK POPLAR

Populus nigra 'Italica'
Zones 3–9

'Instant shade' – tall, narrow and very fast-growing

47B EASTERN COTTONWOOD

Populus deltoides
Zones 2–9

Speedster! The fastest growing species with commercial value in North America

47C PLAINS COTTONWOOD

Populus deltoides ssp. *monlifera*
Zones 3–9

"…shimmering, tremulous leaves (that) are hardly ever quiet, but if the wind stirs at all, rustle and quiver and sigh all day long…"

—Theodore Roosevelt, in Ranch Life and the Hunting Trail

47D RED MULBERRY

Morus rubra
Zones 5–9

Our native mulberry and highly popular with people and wildlife for its blackberry-like fruit

Are the leaves twice as long as wide, tapered at the tip; the bark of the trunk with high, corky ridges? **CLUE:** *The fruit when ripe is purple and a berry-like DRUPE.* It is a **common hackberry.**

YES GO TO 49 A

OR

Are the leaves about as wide as long and heart-shaped; the bark of the trunk without corky ridges? **CLUE:** *The fruit is a small nut attached to a wing-like leaf or BRACT.* These are linden or basswood trees.

Are the leaves 5–6" (12.7–15.2 cm) long? It is an **American basswood (American linden).**

YES GO TO 49 B

OR

Are the leaves 1½–2½" (3.8–6.4 cm) long? It is a **littleleaf linden.**

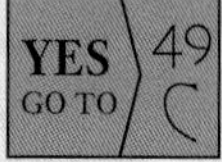

Is the leaf notched or flat across the top edge with buds on stalks? **CLUE:** *The fruit is a small, woody cone.* It is a **European alder.**

YES GO TO 49 D

OR

Is the fruit not small, woody, cone-like and the buds not stalked?

YES GO TO 48 D

Are the leaf bases different on both sides of the PETIOLE, with the leaves flattened horizontally along the twig and the fruit is flattened and winged? These are elm trees.

OR

Are the leaf bases the same on both sides of the PETIOLE?

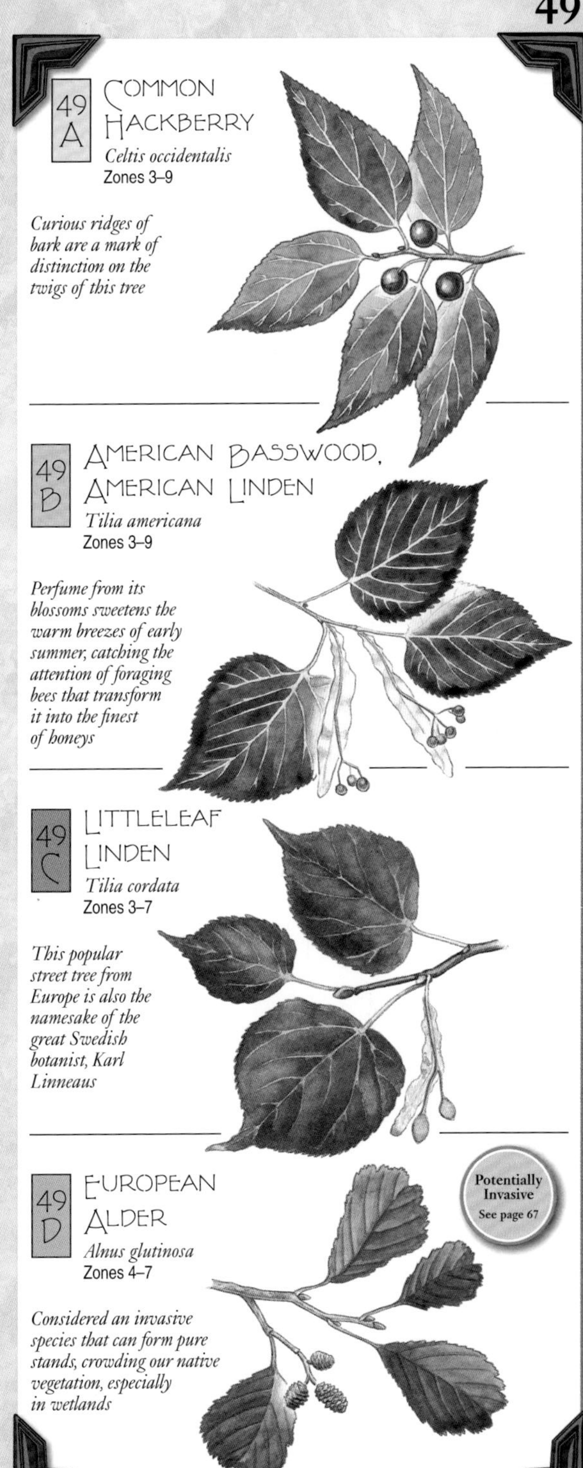
49 A
COMMON HACKBERRY
Celtis occidentalis
Zones 3–9
Curious ridges of bark are a mark of distinction on the twigs of this tree
49 B
AMERICAN BASSWOOD, AMERICAN LINDEN
Tilia americana
Zones 3–9
Perfume from its blossoms sweetens the warm breezes of early summer, catching the attention of foraging bees that transform it into the finest of honeys
49 C
LITTLELEAF LINDEN
Tilia cordata
Zones 3–7
This popular street tree from Europe is also the namesake of the great Swedish botanist, Karl Linneaus
49 D
EUROPEAN ALDER
Alnus glutinosa
Zones 4–7
Potentially Invasive
See page 67
Considered an invasive species that can form pure stands, crowding our native vegetation, especially in wetlands

50

Are the leaves between 3–7" (7.6–17.8 cm) long, with doubly TOOTHED MARGINS? — **YES** GO TO 50 B

OR

Are the leaves ¾–3" (1.9–7.6 cm) long, with only singly TOOTHED MARGINS? **CLUE:** *Their bases may be only slightly different on each side of the PETIOLE.* — **YES** GO TO 50 D

Are the leaves less than 4" (10.2 cm) long with twigs that have corky ridges? It is a **rock elm (cork elm).** — **YES** GO TO 50 F

OR

Are the leaves over 4" (10.2 cm) long with twigs that do not have corky ridges? — **YES** GO TO 50 C

Are the leaves very rough on top? It is a **slippery elm.** — **YES** GO TO 51 A

OR

Are the leaves smooth or slightly rough on top? It is an **American elm.** — **YES** GO TO 51 B

Are the leaves thick, dark green, and shiny on top? **CLUE:** *The fruit matures in the fall.* It is a **Chinese elm.** — **YES** GO TO 51 C

OR

Are the leaves dull green on top, and not thick? **CLUE:** *The fruit matures in the spring.* It is a **Siberian elm.** — **YES** GO TO 51 D

Is the bark on the trunk white to bronze and papery, peeling easily? These are birch trees. — **YES** GO TO 52 A

OR

Is the bark on the trunk not white or papery, and not easy to peel? — **YES** GO TO 52 B

ROCK ELM, CORK ELM

Ulmus thomasii
Zones 3–7

Two well deserved names – rock elm for its very hard wood, and cork elm for the corky wings on older branches

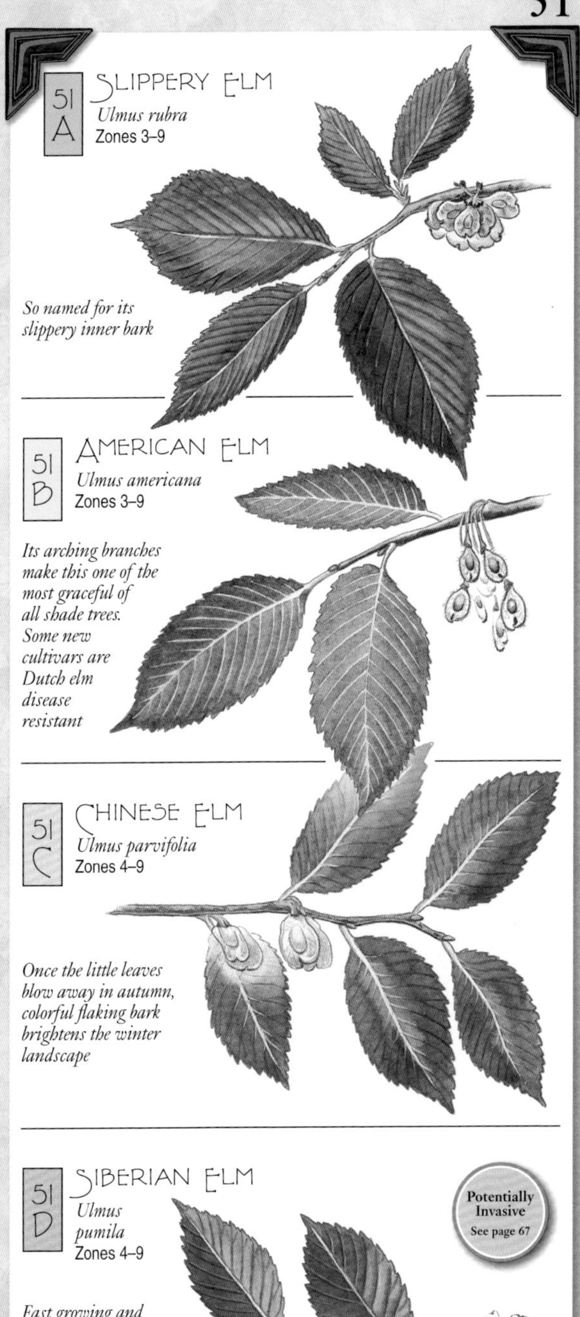

51 A

SLIPPERY ELM

Ulmus rubra
Zones 3–9

So named for its slippery inner bark

51 B

AMERICAN ELM

Ulmus americana
Zones 3–9

Its arching branches make this one of the most graceful of all shade trees. Some new cultivars are Dutch elm disease resistant

51 C

CHINESE ELM

Ulmus parvifolia
Zones 4–9

Once the little leaves blow away in autumn, colorful flaking bark brightens the winter landscape

51 D

SIBERIAN ELM

Ulmus pumila
Zones 4–9

Potentially Invasive
See page 67

Fast growing and disease resistant, but also considered an invasive species

Is the bark on older trunks and branches bright white with black cracks? It is a **paper birch.**

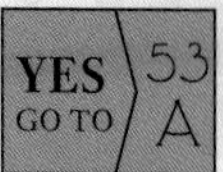

OR

Is the bark on older trunks and branches bronze to cinnamon colored? It is a **river birch.**

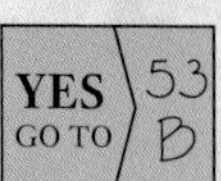

Is the fruit a dry small CAPSULE?

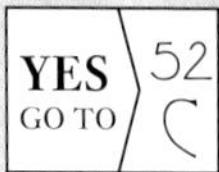

OR

Is the fruit or DRUPE moist and fleshy?

Are the leaves very narrow, at least 4 times as long as wide? These are willow trees.

OR

Are the leaves not as narrow as above?

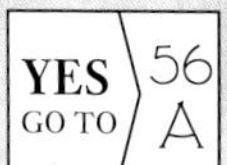

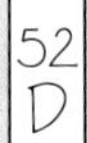

Do the leaves have glands (bumps) where the leaf BLADE meets the PETIOLE? **CLUE:** *The fruit has one stony seed.*

OR

Do the leaves not have glands (bumps) where the leaf BLADE meets the PETIOLE? **CLUE:** *The fruit has several seeds.*

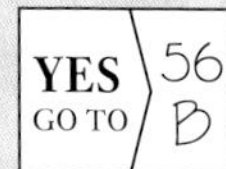

Is the fruit shiny, smooth, and generally 1" (2.5 cm) or less in diameter? These are cherry trees.

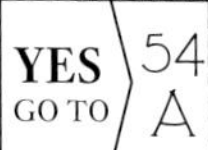

OR

Is the fruit DOWNY and generally more than 1" (2.5 cm) in diameter? These are peach or apricot trees.

Does the tree have long, slender, drooping branches? It is a **weeping willow.**

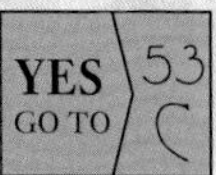

OR

Does the tree not have branches as above? It is a **black willow.**

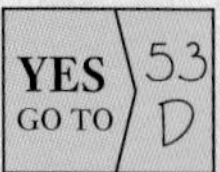

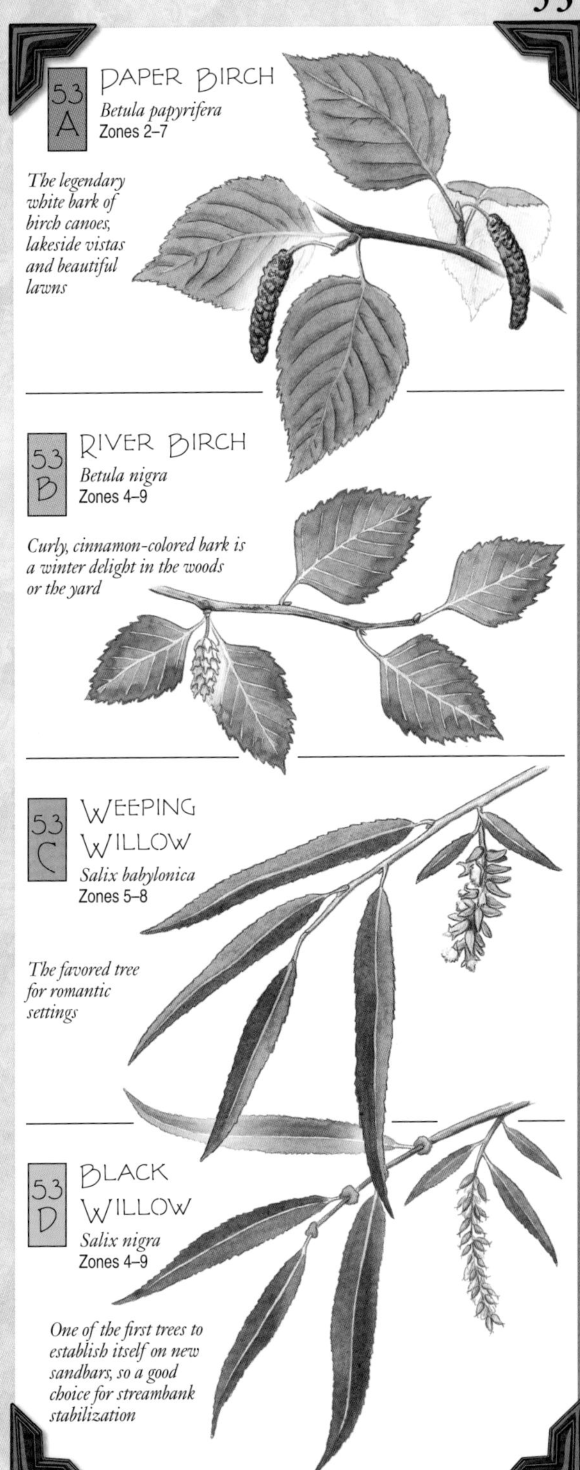
53 A
PAPER BIRCH
Betula papyrifera
Zones 2–7
The legendary white bark of birch canoes, lakeside vistas and beautiful lawns
53 B
RIVER BIRCH
Betula nigra
Zones 4–9
Curly, cinnamon-colored bark is a winter delight in the woods or the yard
53 C
WEEPING WILLOW
Salix babylonica
Zones 5–8
The favored tree for romantic settings
53 D
BLACK WILLOW
Salix nigra
Zones 4–9
One of the first trees to establish itself on new sandbars, so a good choice for streambank stabilization

Are the leaves somewhat thick and leathery? **CLUE:** *The fruit is more than ½" (1.3 cm) in diameter.* It is a **sour cherry.**

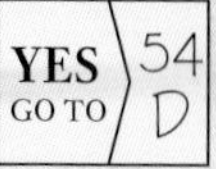

OR

Are the leaves not thick or leathery? **CLUE:** *The fruit is less than ½" (1.3 cm) in diameter.*

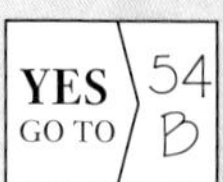

Are the leaves long and narrow (2 or 3 times as long as wide), with brown hairs along the underside of the MIDRIB near the leaf base? **CLUE:** *The fruit is ½" (1.3 cm) or less in diameter and nearly black.* It is a **black cherry.**

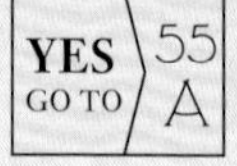

OR

Are the leaves more egg-shaped or oval (2 or less times longer than wide), with no brown hairs? **CLUE:** *The fruit is similar to black cherry but red to purple.* It is a **chokecherry.**

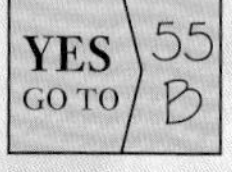

Are the leaves long and narrow (4–6 times as long as wide)? **CLUE:** *The fruit is about 3" (7.6 cm) in diameter.* It is a **peach.**

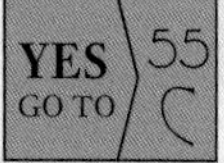

OR

Are the leaves not narrow as above, with smaller fruit? It is an **apricot.**

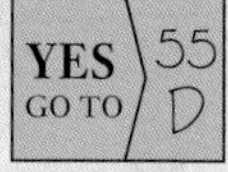

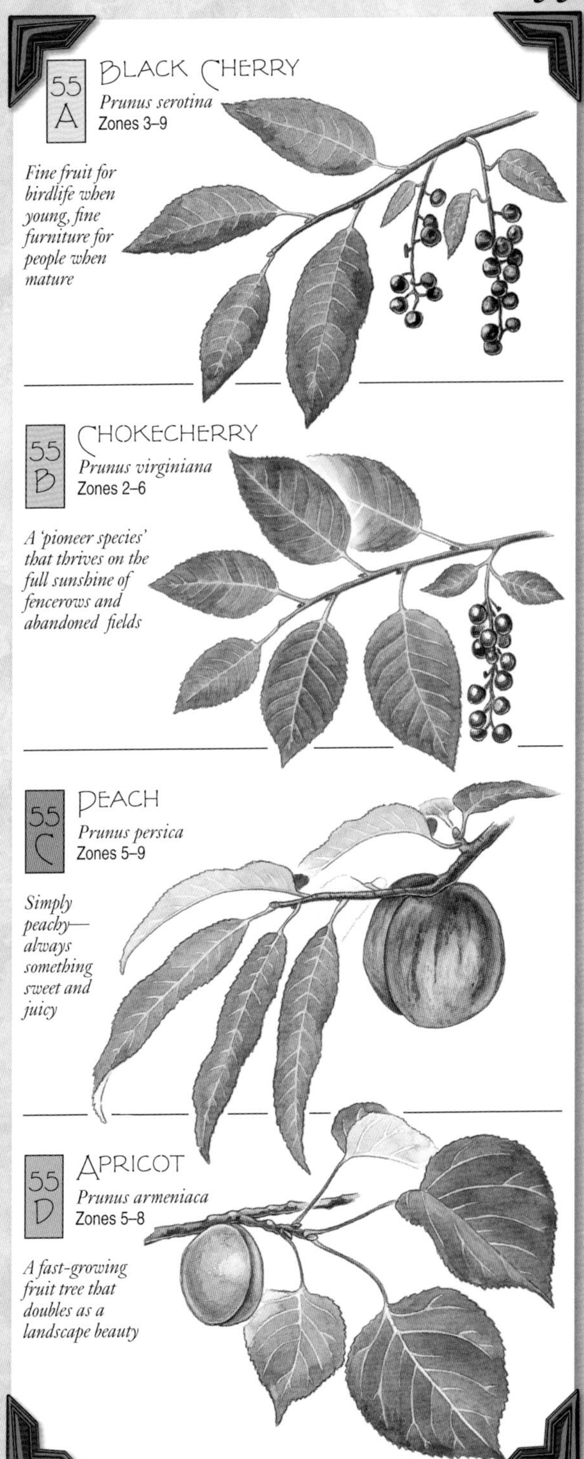

55A Black Cherry

Prunus serotina
Zones 3–9

Fine fruit for birdlife when young, fine furniture for people when mature

55B Chokecherry

Prunus virginiana
Zones 2–6

A 'pioneer species' that thrives on the full sunshine of fencerows and abandoned fields

55C Peach

Prunus persica
Zones 5–9

Simply peachy—always something sweet and juicy

55D Apricot

Prunus armeniaca
Zones 5–8

A fast-growing fruit tree that doubles as a landscape beauty

56

Are the leaf MARGINS sharply double-TOOTHED, leaves usually arranged along the twig in a flattened manner? **CLUE:** *The fruit is in clusters of flattened winged seeds.*

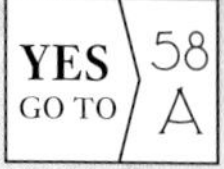

OR

Are the leaf MARGINS finely single-TOOTHED? **CLUE:** *The fruit is a 5-sided CAPSULE in clusters of many.* It is a **sourwood.**

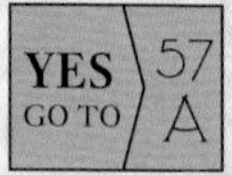

Is the fruit (POME) an apple, ¾" (1.9 cm) or more in diameter?

YES GO TO 56 C

OR

Is the fruit a pear? (Bradford pear branches all curve upward; the small fruit does not look like a common pear). It is a **pear.**

YES GO TO 57 B

OR

Is the fruit similar to an apple, but dark red to purple and ¼–½" (0.6–1.3 cm) in diameter? **CLUE:** *The flowers have 5 long, thin petals that appear very early in the spring.* It is a **downy serviceberry (Juneberry, shadbush).**

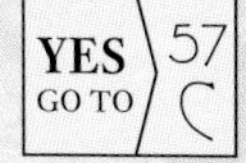

Is the apple 2" (5.1 cm) in diameter or more when mature? It is an **apple.**

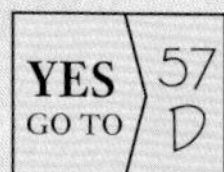

OR

Is the apple less than 2" (5.1 cm) in diameter when mature? It is a **prairie crabapple.**

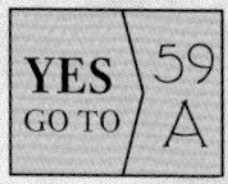

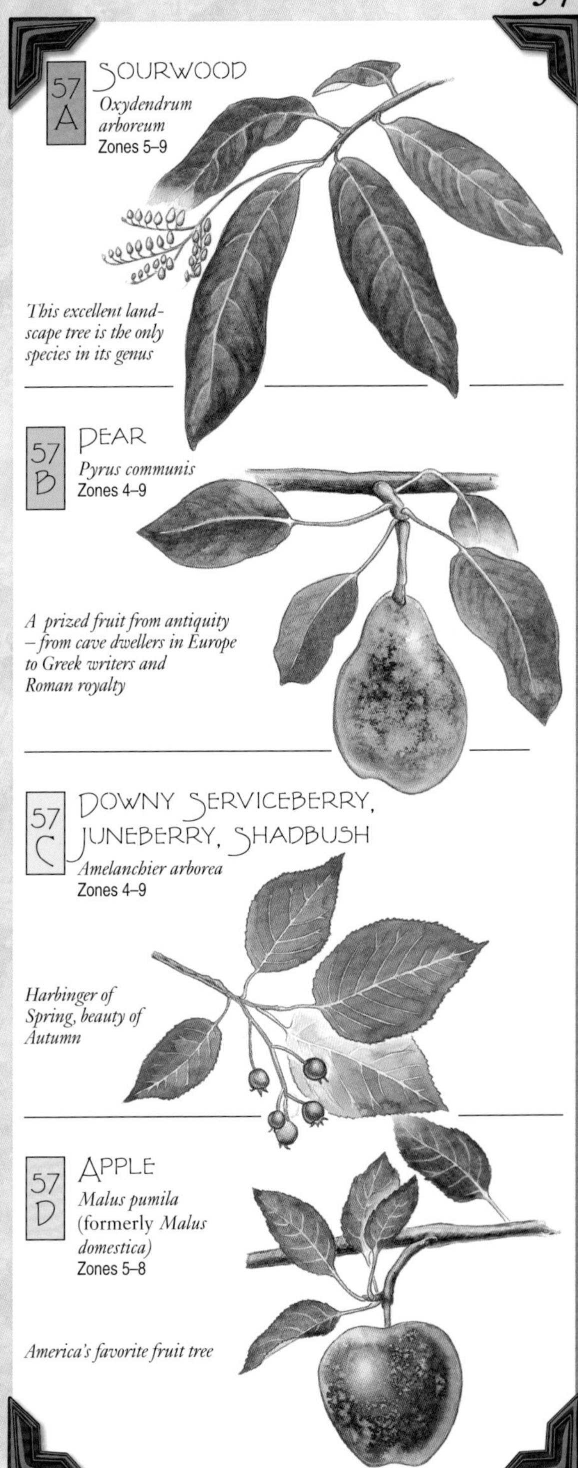

57 A

SOURWOOD

Oxydendrum arboreum
Zones 5–9

This excellent landscape tree is the only species in its genus

57 B

PEAR

Pyrus communis
Zones 4–9

A prized fruit from antiquity – from cave dwellers in Europe to Greek writers and Roman royalty

57 C

DOWNY SERVICEBERRY, JUNEBERRY, SHADBUSH

Amelanchier arborea
Zones 4–9

Harbinger of Spring, beauty of Autumn

57 D

APPLE

Malus pumila (formerly *Malus domestica)*
Zones 5–8

America's favorite fruit tree

Does the tree have smooth, gray bark, with a sinewy stem? It is an **American hornbeam.**

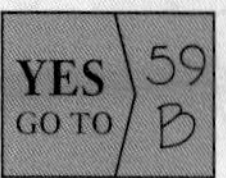

OR

Does the tree have rough, shreddy bark? It is an **eastern hophornbeam.**

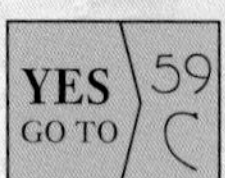

Are the leaves once or twice PINNATELY COMPOUND, BLADES with deeply TOOTHED or LOBED MARGINS? **CLUE:** *The flowers are bright yellow and appear in midsummer.* It is a **goldenraintree.**

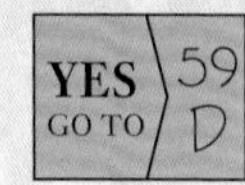

OR

Are the leaves once or twice PINNATELY COMPOUND, BLADES with MARGINS that are not deeply TOOTHED or LOBED?

Are the leaves two or three times PINNATELY COMPOUND (some once COMPOUND on the same tree)?

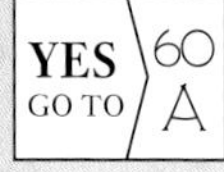

Are the leaves only once COMPOUND?

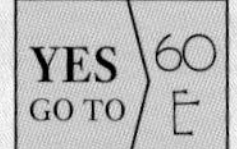

Are the individual BLADES ½" (1.3 cm) long or less? **CLUE:** *The flowers are pink and the fruit is a 5–7" (12.7–17.8 cm) long, brown, thin pod.* It is a **mimosa (silk tree).**

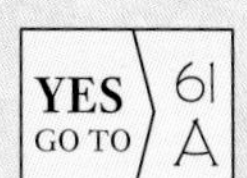

OR

Are the individual BLADES 2–3" (5.1–7.6 cm) long with smooth MARGINS, whole leaves 1–3' (30.5–91.4 cm) long? **CLUE:** *The fruit on the female tree is a 5–10" (12.7–25.4 cm) long brown, leathery pod with ¾" (1.9 cm) seeds.* It is a **Kentucky coffeetree.**

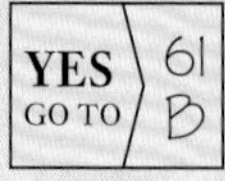

OR

Are the individual BLADES ½–1½" (1.3–3.8 cm) long or less with finely TOOTHED MARGINS and whole leaves 6–12" (15.2–30.5 cm) long? **CLUE:** *Native trees often have stout, branched thorns and fruit that is an 8–18" (20.3–45.7 cm) long, brown, leathery pod with seeds that are the size of watermelon seeds.* It is a **honeylocust.**

YES GO TO 61 B

59 A

Prairie Crabapple

Malus ioensis
Zones 4–7

Fruits that are hard and sour, but with flowers showy and fragrant

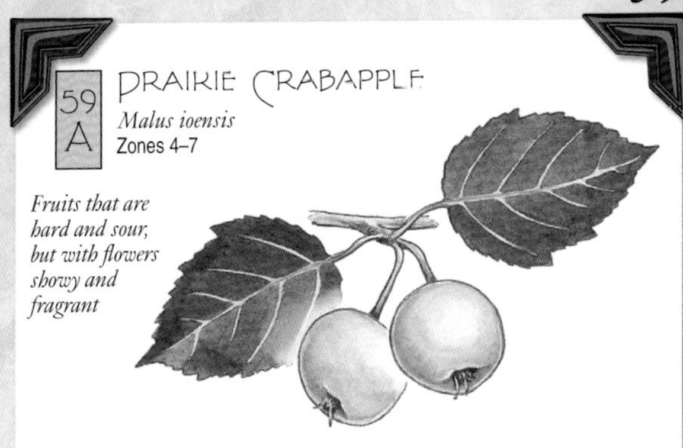

59 B

American Hornbeam

Carpinus caroliniana
Zones 3–9

A little tree with bark appearing as muscles and covering very hard wood

59 C

Eastern Hophornbeam

Ostrya virginiana
Zones 3–9

Small in stature but mighty in strength, with wood like its alternate name – ironwood

59 D

Goldenraintree

Koelreuteria paniculata
Zones 5–9

Flowers of gold and fruits like tiny Chinese lanterns

Are the side buds hidden by the leaf base? **CLUE:** *The fruit is a LEGUME (pod).*

OR

Are the side buds exposed? **CLUE:** *The fruit is not a LEGUME (pod).*

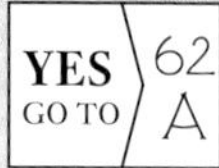

Are the BLADES or leaflets large, 2–4" (5.1–10.2 cm) long? It is a **yellowwood.**

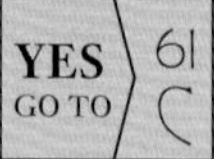

OR

Are the BLADES or leaflets small, less than 2" (5.1 cm) long?

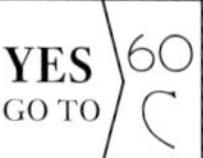

Is the fruit an 8–18" (20.3–45.7 cm) long, brown, leathery pod; native trees having long, branched thorns? It is a **honeylocust.**

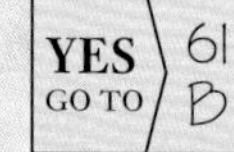

OR

Is the fruit a pod less than 7" (17.8 cm) long, and are there no branched thorns?

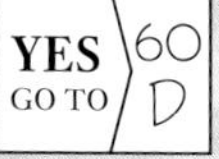

Are the BLADE tips angled and no spines or prickles can be found on twigs? It is a **Japanese pagodatree.**

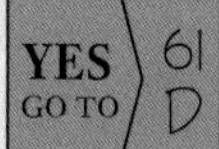

OR

Are BLADE tips rounded and spines or prickles usually present on twigs? It is a **black locust.**

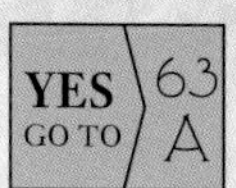

61 A

KENTUCKY COFFEETREE

Gymnocladus dioicus
Zones 3–8

Their double-compound form gives these leaves the distinction of being the largest in eastern North America

61 B

HONEYLOCUST

Gleditsia triacanthos
Zones 3–9

Branching thorns and doubly-compound leaves make this one of our more interesting trees. Gleditsia triacanthos inermis is a thornless honeylocust

61 C

YELLOWWOOD

Cladrastis kentukea
Zones 4–8

Yellow heartwood and yellow fall color gave this rare eastern tree its name

61 D

JAPANESE PAGODATREE

Styphnolobium japonicum (formerly *Sophora japonica*)
Zones 4–7

Like a pleasant surprise, flowers bloom late in the summer long after most other trees, and then leave a blanket of snowy white petals beneath the tree.

62 A

Are the whole leaves 18–36" (45.7–91.4 cm) long, with 11–41 BLADES that give off a strong, musty, unpleasant odor when crushed? **CLUE:** *The fruit is a SAMARA.* It is a **tree-of-heaven.**

SAMARA

YES GO TO 63 B

OR

Are the leaves generally shorter, without a musty, unpleasant odor when crushed? **CLUE:** *The fruit is not a SAMARA.*

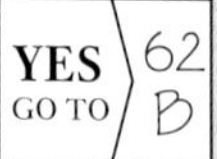
YES GO TO 62 B

---

62 B

Are the BLADE edges coarsely TOOTHED? **CLUE:** *The fruit is ¼–½" (0.6–1.3 cm) in diameter, bright orange-red, and berry-like.*

YES GO TO 62 C

OR

Are the BLADE edges finely TOOTHED? **CLUE:** *The fruit is a nut.*

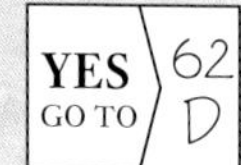
YES GO TO 62 D

---

62 C

Are the BLADES 2–4" (5.1–10.2 cm) long and the buds gummy? It is an **American mountainash.**

YES GO TO 63 C

OR

Are the BLADES 1–2" (2.5–5.1 cm) long and the buds DOWNY? It is a **European mountainash.**

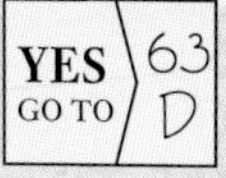
YES GO TO 63 D

62 D

Does the husk of the nut not split along lines when ripe? **CLUE:** *The PITH or center of the twigs is divided into empty chambers by plates.*

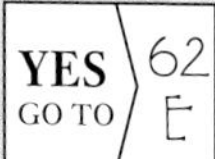
YES GO TO 62 E

OR

Does the husk of the nut split along lines when ripe? **CLUE:** *The PITH or center of the twigs is solid.*

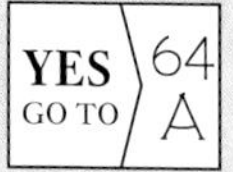
YES GO TO 64 A

62 E

Is the nut spherical and round, the bark dark brown to black and chocolate-brown when cut or broken? **CLUE:** *The PITH is light brown.* It is a **black walnut.**

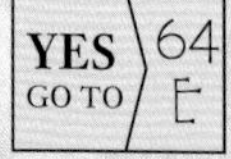
YES GO TO 64 E

OR

Is the nut oblong or oval, the bark gray? **CLUE:** *The PITH is dark brown.* It is a **butternut.**

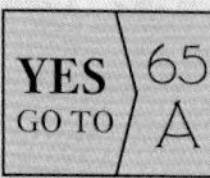
YES GO TO 65 A

63 A BLACK LOCUST

Robinia pseudoacacia
Zones 4–9

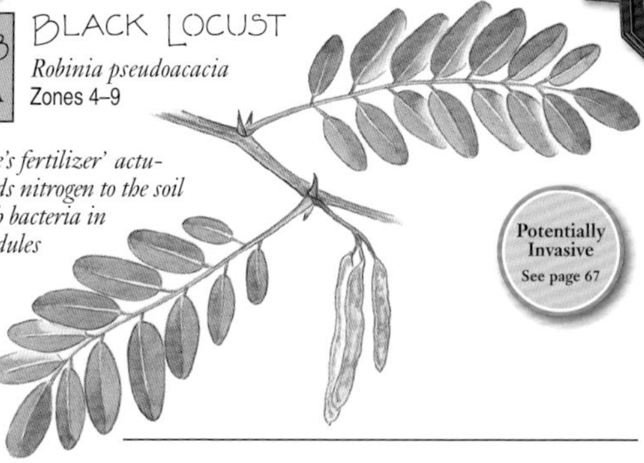

'Nature's fertilizer' actually adds nitrogen to the soil through bacteria in root nodules

Potentially Invasive
See page 67

63 B TREE-OF-HEAVEN

Ailanthus altissima
Zones 4–8

Potentially Invasive
See page 67

The scientific name of this exotic means "tree reaching for the sky"

63 C AMERICAN MOUNTAINASH

Sorbus americana
Zones 2–7

Denizen of swamps and low, moist woodlands

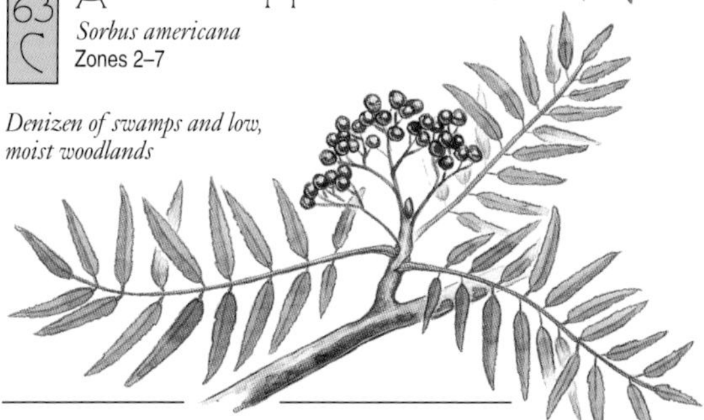

63 D EUROPEAN MOUNTAINASH

Sorbus aucuparia
Zones 3–6

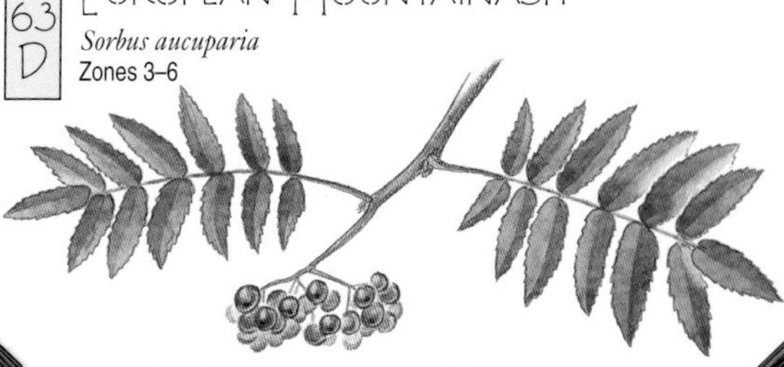

A deep freeze makes its pretty red fruits more palatable to birds

64

Do the whole leaves have 9–17 BLADES, with the one at the tip about the same size as the others? It is a **pecan.**

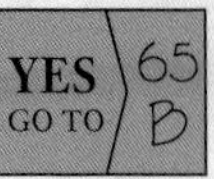

OR

Do the leaves usually have 5–9 BLADES, with the one at the tip often larger than the others?

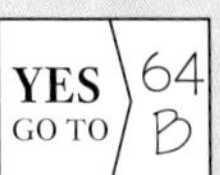

Do the leaves usually have 5, but sometimes 7 BLADES?

OR

Do the leaves usually have 7–9 (occasionally 11) BLADES?

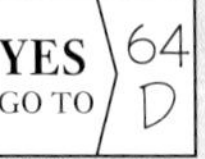

Is the husk on the nut thick (¼–½" or 0.6–1.3 cm), splitting completely when ripe to release the nut; with the bark on older trees peeling in long, shaggy sections? It is a **shagbark hickory.**

YES GO TO 65 C

OR

Is the pear-shaped husk on the nut thin (less than ⅛" or 0.125 cm), often splitting only part way to the base; with the bark on older trees tight with rounded ridges, not shaggy? It is a **pignut hickory.**

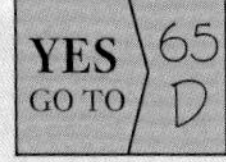

Are the buds sulfur-yellow, with the fruit husk thin and the nut shell thin? It is a **bitternut hickory.**

YES GO TO 66 B

OR

Are the buds not sulfur-yellow, with the fruit husk thick and the nut shell thick?

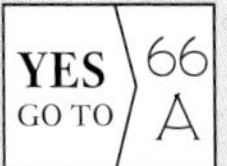

Gunstocks, fine furniture and delicious nuts – this tree was a boon to the pioneers and is one of our most valuable trees today

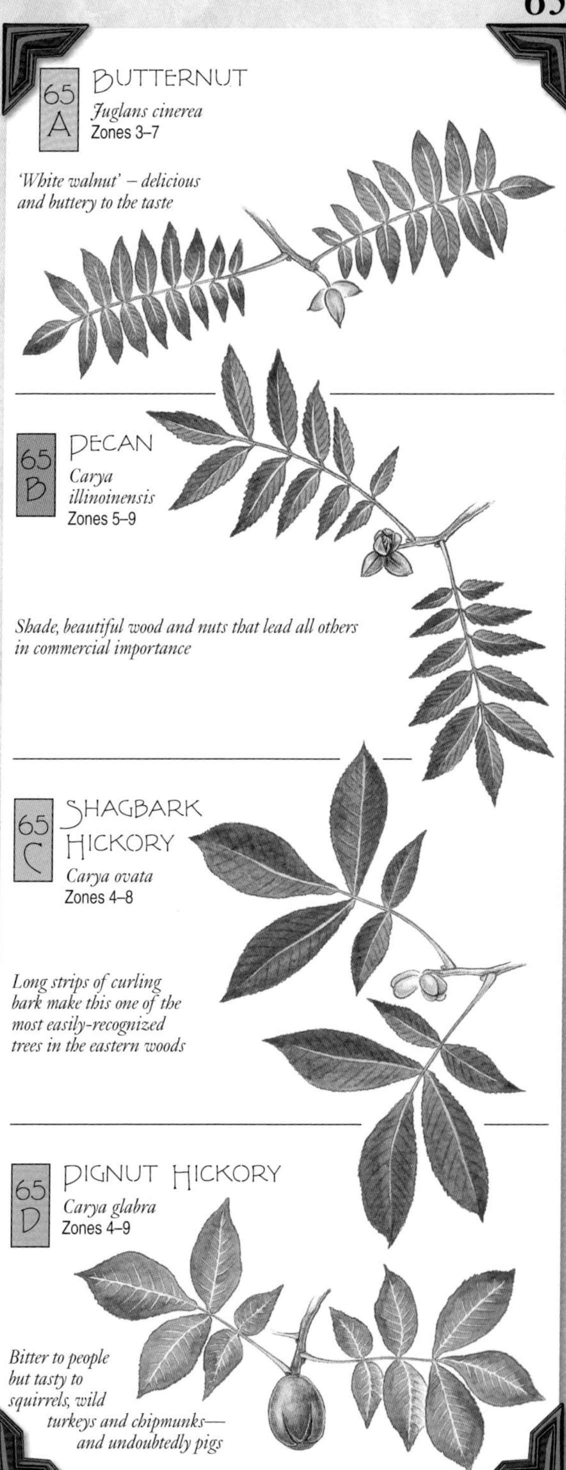
65 A
BUTTERNUT
Juglans cinerea
Zones 3–7
'White walnut' – delicious and buttery to the taste
65 B
PECAN
Carya illinoinensis
Zones 5–9
Shade, beautiful wood and nuts that lead all others in commercial importance
65 C
SHAGBARK HICKORY
Carya ovata
Zones 4–8
Long strips of curling bark make this one of the most easily-recognized trees in the eastern woods
65 D
PIGNUT HICKORY
Carya glabra
Zones 4–9
Bitter to people but tasty to squirrels, wild turkeys and chipmunks— and undoubtedly pigs

Is the fruit husk ¼–½" (0.6–1.3 cm) thick, the nut with 4–6-ribs, and the bark on older trunks broken into long, shaggy sections? It is a **shellbark hickory.**

YES GO TO 66 C

OR

Is the fruit husk ⅛–¼" (0.125–0.6 cm) thick, the nut 4-ribbed, and the bark on older trunks ridged and furrowed, not shaggy? **CLUE:** *Only hickory with short soft hairs on undersides of leaves and stems.* It is a **mockernut hickory.**

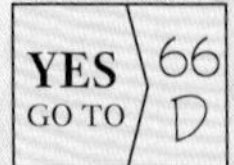

66 B

BITTERNUT HICKORY

Carya cordiformis
Zones 4–9

The most common and most widely distributed of the hickory species

66 C

SHELLBARK HICKORY

Carya laciniosa
Zones 5–8

Flood plains and bottomlands are the natural home of this tree with a nut favored by humans and wildlife

66 D

MOCKERNUT HICKORY

Carya tomentosa
Zones 4–9

Don't be fooled (mocked!) by the large fruits, as only small nuts will be found inside the very thick shell.

This symbol indicates that a tree is potentially invasive.

Invasive plants are known to reproduce rapidly and quickly spread over large areas of land. They have few natural controls such as herbivores or diseases to stop their spread and they can threaten biological diversity.

Contact your local County Cooperative Extension Agent or State Forester to learn about invasive trees and plants in your area.

21C: NORWAY MAPLE
Acer platanoides

27C: WHITE POPLAR
Populus alba

31B, 48E: WHITE MULBERRY
Morus alba

35D: RUSSIAN OLIVE
Elaegnus angustifolia

49D: EUROPEAN ADLER
Alnus glutinosa

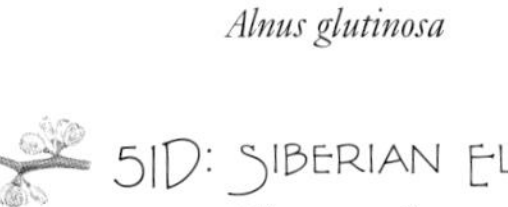

51D: SIBERIAN ELM
Ulmus pumila

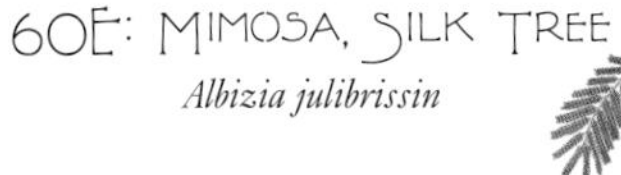

60E: MIMOSA, SILK TREE
Albizia julibrissin

63A: BLACK LOCUST
Robina pseudoacacia

63B: TREE-OF-HEAVEN
Ailanthus altissima

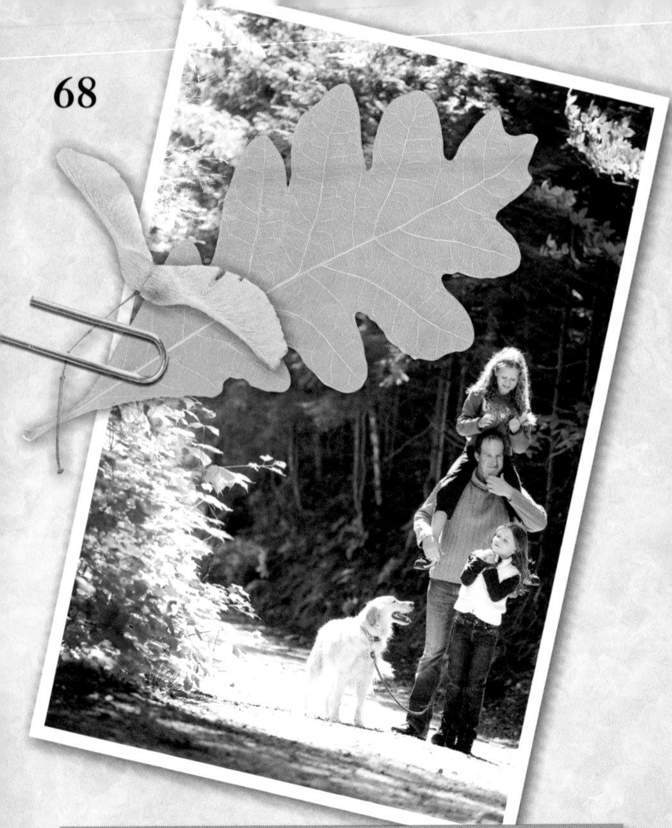

WESTERN START HERE

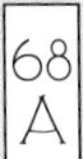

68 A Does the tree bear cones and have leaves that are needle-like? **CLUE:** *These trees are called CONIFERS (cone-bearing) and most are EVERGREEN (trees with needles or leaves that remain alive and on the tree through the winter and into the next growing season).*

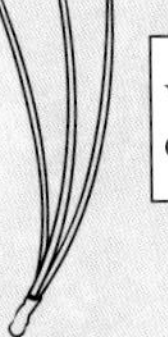

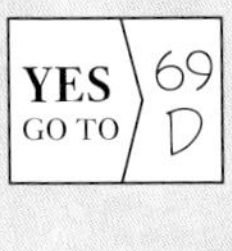

YES GO TO **69 D**

OR

Does the tree have scale-like, or awl-shaped leaves, usually EVERGREEN, sometimes reduced to a thick fleshy stem?

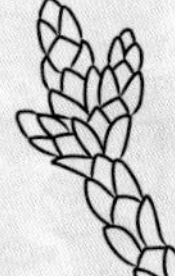

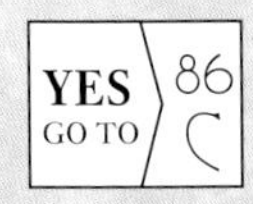

YES GO TO **86 C**

OR

Does the tree have leaves that are flat and thin? **CLUE:** *These trees are called BROADLEAF, (a tree with leaves that are flat and thin) and bear a variety of fruit and flowers. Most are DECIDUOUS (shedding all leaves annually).*

YES GO TO **69 A**

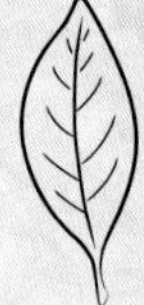

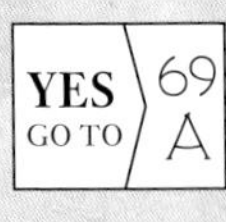

69A

Are the leaves SIMPLE (one BLADE attached to a stalk or PETIOLE)?

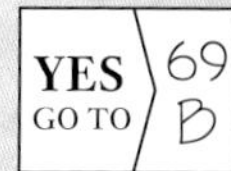

OR

Are the leaves COMPOUND (more than one BLADE attached to a single stalk or PETIOLE)?

OR

Are the uniquely fan-shaped leaves mostly attached, in clusters, to short, SPUR-like branches? It is a **ginkgo.**

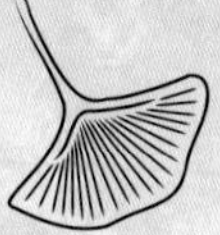

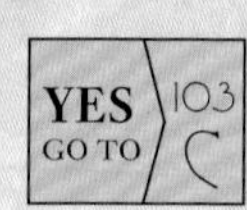

Are the SIMPLE leaves OPPOSITE (2 leaves that are directly across from each other on the same twig)?

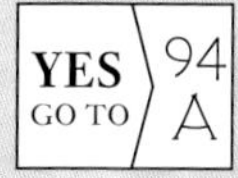

OR

Are the SIMPLE leaves ALTERNATE (leaves that are staggered, not opposite each other on the twig)?

Are the COMPOUND leaves OPPOSITE?

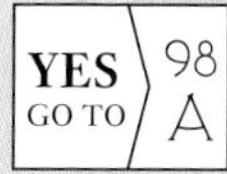

OR

Are the COMPOUND leaves ALTERNATE?

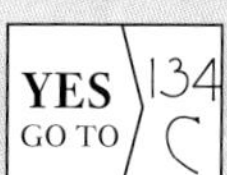

Are the needles arranged mostly in clusters of 2–5 and EVERGREEN? These are pine trees.

OR

Are the needles DECIDUOUS, 1–1½" (2.5–3.8 cm) long, and mostly arranged in clusters of many on short, SPUR-like branches? **CLUE:** *Cones are upright and 1" (2.5 cm) long.* It is a **western larch.**

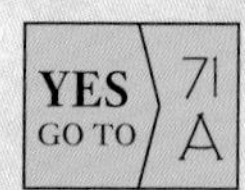

OR

Are the needles arranged singly, less than 2" (5.1 cm) long; cones 1–2" (2.5–5.1 cm) long with a few thick, often prickly scales; and large, edible, wingless seeds? **CLUE:** *The tree is native in scattered areas from southern Idaho to Mexico.* It is a **singleleaf pinyon.**

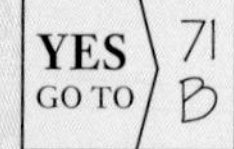

OR

Are the needles arranged singly and EVERGREEN but different than above?

70

Are the needles mainly clustered in groups of 2–4, the cone scales thick and often prickly?

OR

Are the needles mainly clustered in groups of 5, the cone scales usually without prickles?

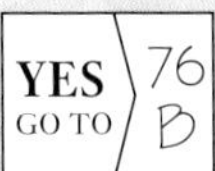

Are the needles generally less than 2" (5.1 cm) long and in groups of 1–4; the cones 1–2" (2.5–5.1 cm) long with few scales; the edible seeds large and without wings? These are pinyon pines.

OR

Are the needles generally more than 2" (5.1 cm) long and in groups of 2–3; the cones longer than 2" (5.1 cm) with many scales; the seed size varies?

Are the needles usually held singly? **CLUE:** *Native in scattered areas from southern Idaho to Mexico, this is the only single-needled pine in the world.* It is a **singleleaf pinyon.**

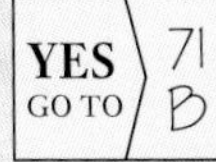

OR

Are the needles mostly clustered in groups of 2 (occasionally 1's or 3's)? **CLUE:** *The tree is native throughout parts of the Southwest.* It is a **pinyon (piñón, Colorado pinyon).**

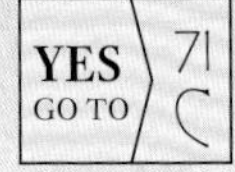

OR

Are the needles mostly clustered in groups of 4? **CLUE:** *The tree is native only to the mountains of southern California.* It is a **Parry pinyon.**

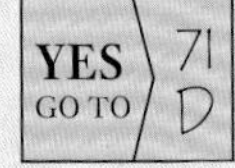

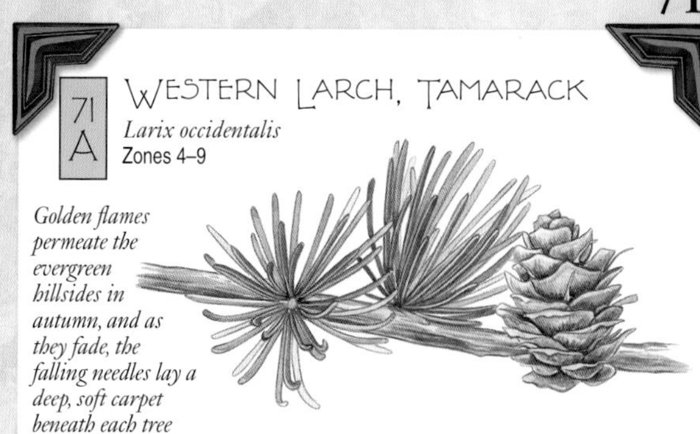

71A WESTERN LARCH, TAMARACK

Larix occidentalis
Zones 4–9

Golden flames permeate the evergreen hillsides in autumn, and as they fade, the falling needles lay a deep, soft carpet beneath each tree

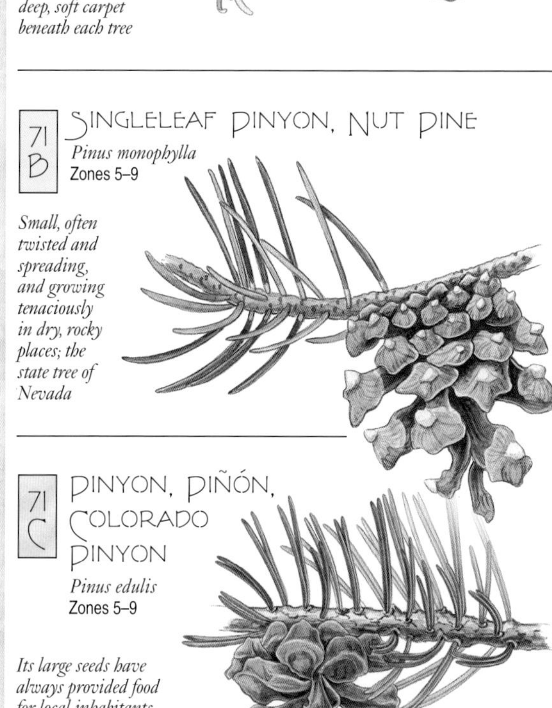

71B SINGLELEAF PINYON, NUT PINE

Pinus monophylla
Zones 5–9

Small, often twisted and spreading, and growing tenaciously in dry, rocky places; the state tree of Nevada

71C PINYON, PIÑÓN, COLORADO PINYON

Pinus edulis
Zones 5–9

Its large seeds have always provided food for local inhabitants and continue popular today as 'pine nuts'

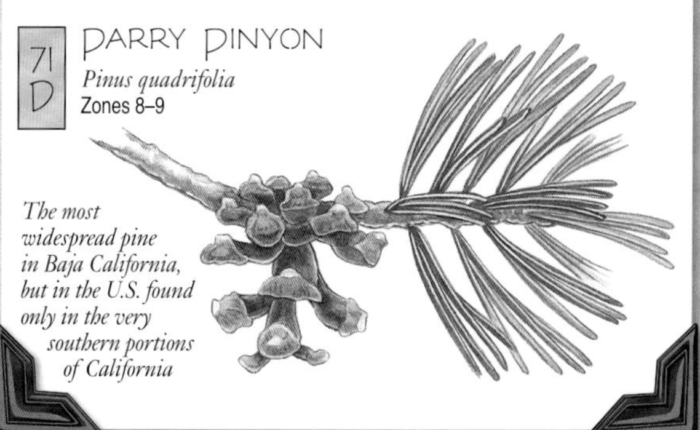

71D PARRY PINYON

Pinus quadrifolia
Zones 8–9

The most widespread pine in Baja California, but in the U.S. found only in the very southern portions of California

Are the needles mainly clustered in groups of 3?

OR

Are the needles mainly clustered in groups of 2?

OR

Are the needles 4–7" (10.2–17.8 cm) long, clustered in groups of 2 and 3 on the same tree? **CLUE:** *The cones are armed with short stout prickles.* It is a **ponderosa pine.**

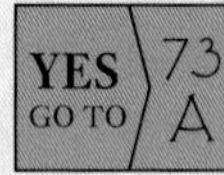

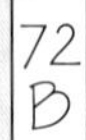

Are the cones large and heavy, with long, curved, claw-like spines? **CLUE:** *This tree is only native to California.*

OR

Are the cones not large and heavy, without long, curved, claw-like spines?

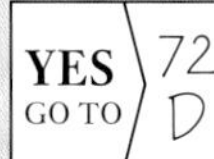

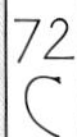

Are the needles flexible; the cones 6–10" (15.2–25.4 cm) long; the seeds longer than the flat, paper-like wings surrounding them? It is a **gray pine.**

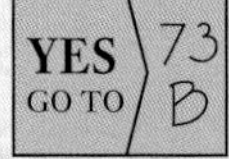

OR

Are the needles stiff; the cones 10–14" (25.4–35.6 cm) long; the seeds shorter than the flat, paper-like wings surrounding them? It is a **Coulter pine.**

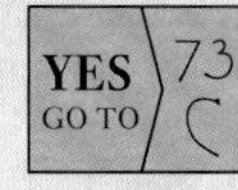

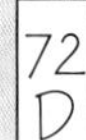

Are the cones asymmetrical with thickened scales, often remaining closed and attached to the tree for many years?

OR

Are the cones symmetrical, with thinner scales?

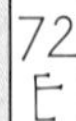

Are the ends of the cone scales flattened or faceted with a pyramid-like shape? Cones can remain on tree for its entire lifetime. **CLUE:** *This tree is only found in dry foothills in California and Oregon.* It is a **knobcone pine.**

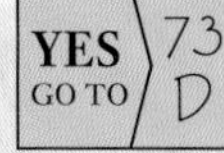

OR

Are the ends of the cone scales rounded and dome-like? **CLUE:** *This tree is rare and found only along the central California and Baja California coasts.* It is a **Monterey pine.**

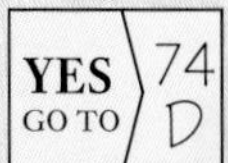

73A

PONDEROSA PINE

Pinus ponderosa
Zones 3–7

Legendary tree of the West – and widely distributed north to south and low to high

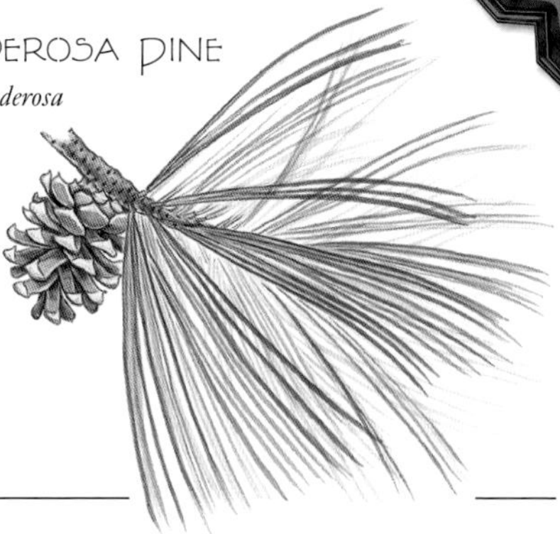

73B

GRAY PINE

Pinus sabiniana
Zones 8–9

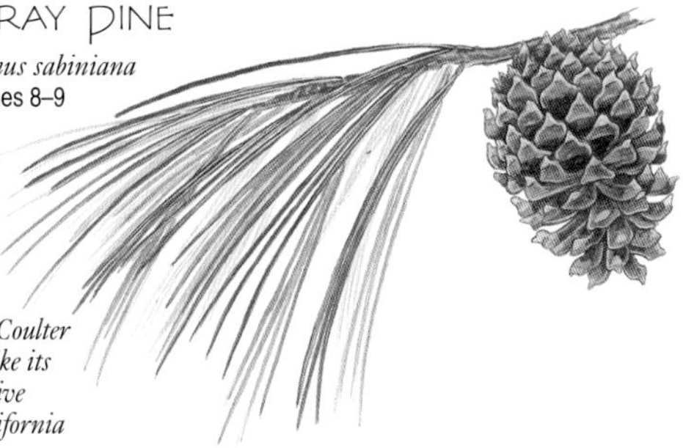

Similar to Coulter pine, and like its cousin, native only to California

73C

COULTER PINE

Pinus coulteri
Zones 8–9

Our tree with the heaviest cones in the world—sometimes weighing as much as five pounds!

73D

KNOBCONE PINE

Pinus attenuata
Zones 7–8

Tight, prickly cones open after the heat of a forest fire

Are the needles 2–4" (5.1–10.2 cm) long; cones long-stalked, 1½–2" (3.8–5.1 cm) long, maturing in 3 years? It is a **Chihuahua pine.**

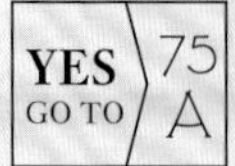

OR

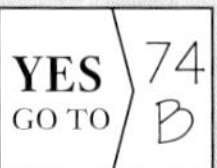

Are the needles over 4" (10.2 cm) long; the cones short-stalked, 2–14" (5.1–35.6 cm) long, maturing in 2 years?

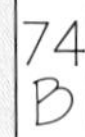

Are the needles 4–9" (10.2–22.9 cm) long; the cones 5–15" (12.7–38.1 cm) long? **CLUE**: *The twigs are purplish.* It is a **Jeffrey pine.**

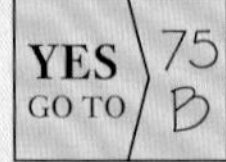

OR

Are the needles 8–15" (20.3–38.1 cm) long; the cones 3–6" (7.6–15.2 cm) long? **CLUE**: *The twigs are orange to red-brown.* It is an **Apache pine.**

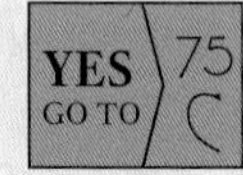

Are the cones symmetrical, with rounded scales, falling shortly after maturity? **CLUE**: *This tree is not native but is fairly widely planted.* It is an **Austrian pine**.

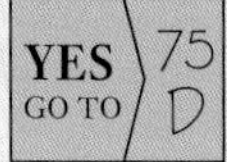

OR

Are the cones asymmetrical, with scales armed with a sharp spine, often remaining closed and attached to the tree for many years? **CLUE**: *This tree is native in various parts of the West.*

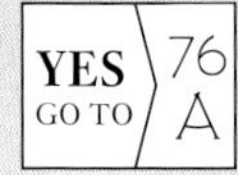

Chihuahua Pine

Pinus leiophylla var. *chihuahuana*
Zones 7–8

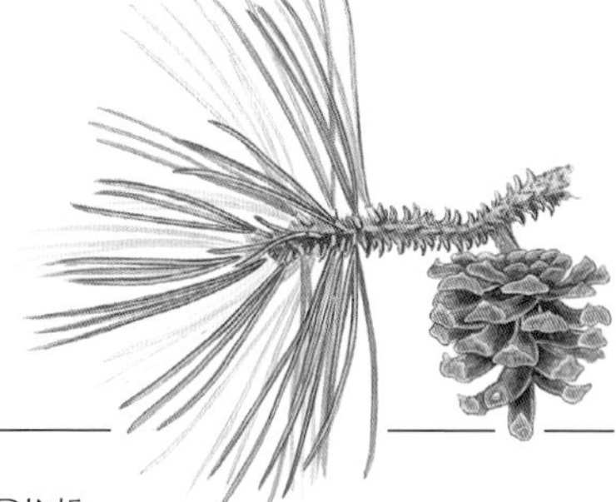

Other than in Mexico, this tree is found growing naturally only in small portions of Arizona and New Mexico; and has the ability to re-sprout after fires – a rare feature among pines

Jeffrey Pine

Pinus jeffreyi
Zones 5–9

Once thought to be a variety of ponderosa pine which it closely resembles, but it is different chemically, ecologically and – if you look closely – physically

Apache Pine

Pinus engelmannii
Zones 8–9

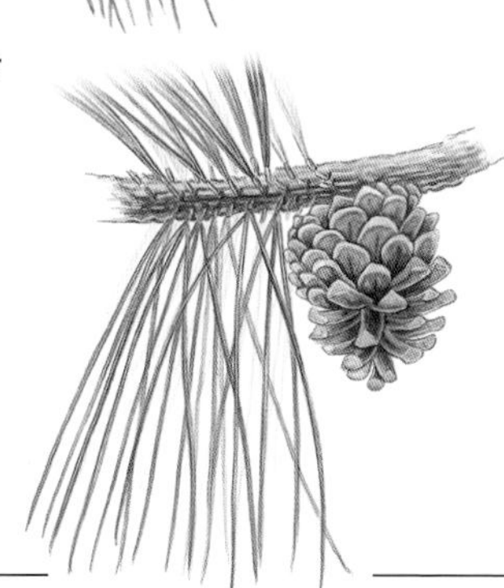

Mostly a pine of Mexico, but enters the U.S. in southwestern New Mexico and southeastern Arizona

Austrian Pine

Pinus nigra
Zones 4–7

From southern Europe and Asia minor to widespread planting in our country on sites where only the drought-tolerant can thrive

76

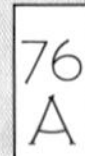

Are the needles 1–3" (2.5–7.6 cm) long? **CLUE:** *This tree is native throughout the West.* It is a **lodgepole pine.**

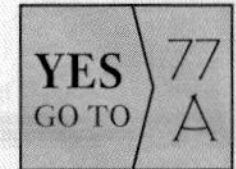

OR

Are the needles 4–7" (10.2–17.8 cm) long? **CLUE:** *This tree is native only to a few scattered locations along the California and Baja California coasts.* It is a **Bishop pine.**

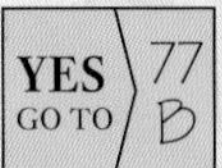

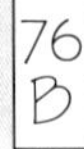

Are the needles 8–13" (20.3–33 cm) long? **CLUE:** *The tree is native only to Santa Rosa Island and a small area north of San Diego, California.* It is a **Torrey pine.**

OR

Are the needles generally less than 4" (10.2 cm) long?

Are the needles slender and 2–4" (5.1–10.2 cm) long; the cone scales thin and without prickles?

OR

Are the needles stout and 1–3" (2.5–7.6 cm) long; the cone scales thick, with or without prickles?

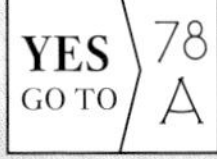

Are the cones 8–11" (20.3–27.9 cm) long with flexible scales? **CLUE:** *This tree is native from California north into Canada.* It is a **western white pine.**

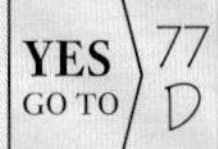

OR

Are the cones 12–26" (30.5–65 cm) long with slightly stiffer scales? **CLUE:** *This tree is native from California north only into Oregon.* It is a **sugar pine.**

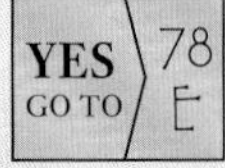

LODGEPOLE PINE

Pinus contorta
Zones 4–9

Pure stands are the result of previous fires, often bringing about tree cover as thick as "the hair on a dog's back"

BISHOP PINE

Pinus muricata
Zones 8–9

The patchy distribution of this species along California's coast is believed to show it was part of an ancient, prehistoric forest.

TORREY PINE

Pinus torreyana
Zone 9

Found naturally only in the coastal chaparral of San Diego County, California, this is our rarest pine species

---

WESTERN WHITE PINE

Pinus monticola
Zones 5–8

Beautiful, straight and tall, once commonly growing to over 200 feet in height; the state tree of Idaho

Are the needles 1½–3" (3.8–7.6 cm) long; cone scales without prickles?

OR

Are the needles 1–1½" (2.5–3.8 cm) long with prickly cone scales?

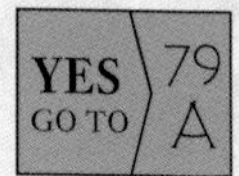

Are the cones 1½–3" (3.8–7.6 cm) long, closed at maturity, disintegrating to release seeds? It is a **whitebark pine.**

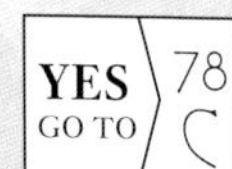

OR

Are the cones 3–10" (7.6–25.4 cm) long and open at maturity?

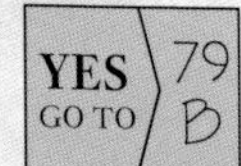

Are the cone scales not strongly turned downward; young branches very flexible? **CLUE:** *This tree is scattered throughout the West.* It is a **limber pine.**

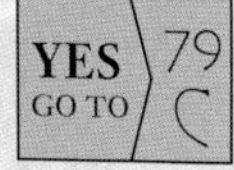

OR

Are the cone scales strongly turned downward? **CLUE:** *The tree is native only along the Mexican border.* It is a **southwestern white pine.**

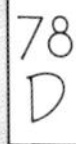

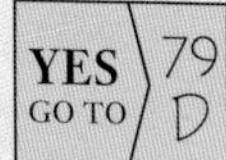

Do the cones have long, slender prickles? **CLUE:** *The tree is native from Colorado to eastern California.* It is a **bristlecone pine.**

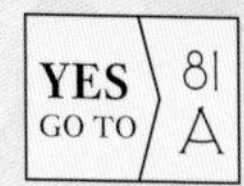

OR

Do the cones have shorter, curved prickles? **CLUE:** *The tree is native only to California.* It is a **foxtail pine.**

78 E

SUGAR PINE

Pinus lambertiana

Zones 6–7

David Douglas, the first person to describe sugar pine in the scientific literature, called it "the most princely of the genus," and was justly amazed by the size of its huge cones

WHITEBARK PINE

Pinus albicaulis
Zones 3–5

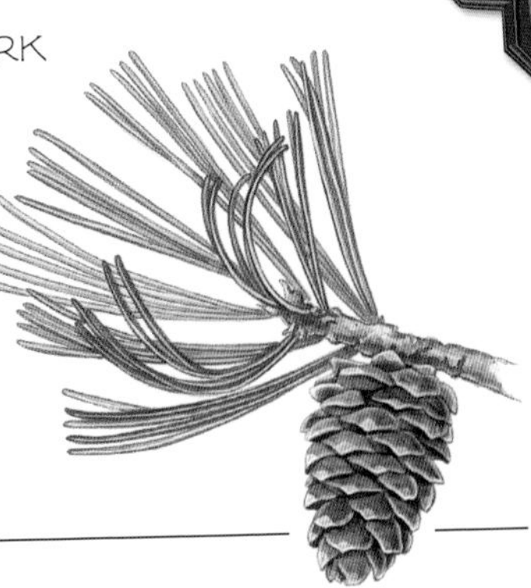

Usually the pine found highest in the Rocky Mountains and Cascades, often among the dwarfed vegetation at treeline

LIMBER PINE

Pinus flexilis
Zones 4-7

So much like whitebark pine that it requires the cones or pollen cones ("flowers") in order to tell them apart

SOUTHWESTERN WHITE PINE

Pinus strobiformis
Zones 5–7

Beautiful, soft foliage covers this drought-tolerant member of the white pine group

BRISTLECONE PINE

Pinus longaeva/Pinus aristata
Zones 4–7

One of the oldest living trees on earth, including "Methuselah," at more than 4,840 years of age

Is the fruit a woody or papery cone of scales with seeds?

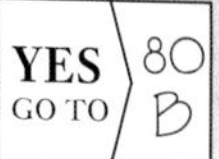

OR

Is the fruit moist and fleshy holding a single seed?

YES GO TO 86 B

Are the cone scales woody and shield-shaped, the cone ¾–1" (1.9–2.5 cm) long, and the tree often very large? **CLUE:** *The tree is only native along the Pacific coast from central California to southern Oregon.* It is a **redwood.**

YES GO TO 81 B

OR

Are the cone scales thin and not shield-shaped?

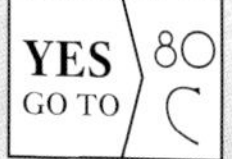

Are the needles held on the twig on peg-like projections that persist after the needle falls?

YES GO TO 80 D

OR

Are the needles not held on the twig on peg-like projections?

Are the needles stalked, blunt, usually difficult to roll between your fingers, flat in cross-section or somewhat rounded? These are hemlock trees.

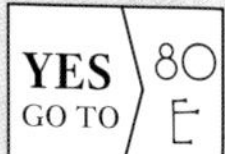

OR

Are the needles not stalked, fairly sharply pointed, usually easy to roll between your fingers, 4-sided or diamond-shaped in cross-section or somewhat flattened in one species? These are spruce trees.

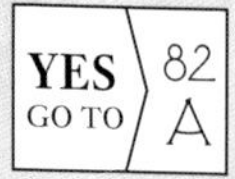

Are the flattened needles grooved on top; the brown cones ½–1" (1.3–2.5 cm) long? It is a **western hemlock.**

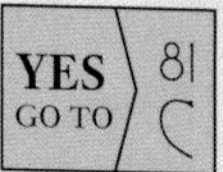

OR

Are the needles rounded on top; spreading in all directions; the cones ¾–3½" (1.9–8.9 cm) long and yellow-green to purple? It is a **mountain hemlock.**

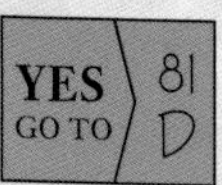

81 A

Foxtail Pine

Pinus balfouriana
Zones 6–9

A rare, high mountain native of California with needles all around the branch appearing like a fox's tail

81 B

Redwood

Sequoia sempervirens
Zones 7–9

Majestic residents of the foggy coastal forests of the West, sometimes towering over 360 feet in the air

81 C

Western Hemlock

Tsuga heterophylla
Zones 6–9

Look for the droopy new growth at the top of this tree

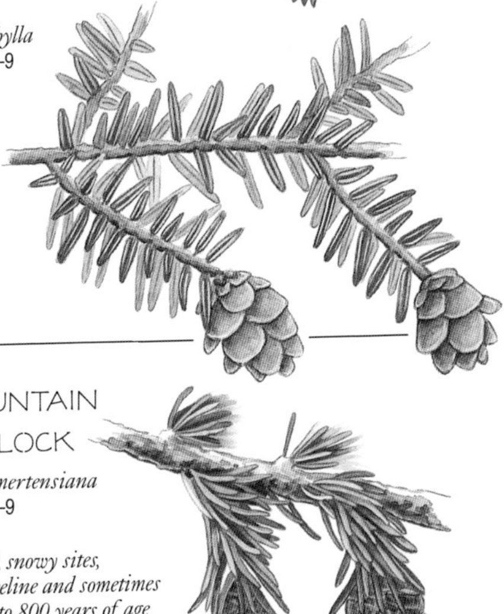

81 D

Mountain Hemlock

Tsuga mertensiana
Zones 4–9

At home on cold, snowy sites, sometimes at treeline and sometimes growing slowly to 800 years of age

Are the cone scales broad, flexible, smooth edged and rounded at the tip? It is a **white spruce** (**Blackhills spruce**).

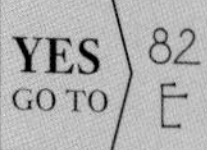

OR

Are the cone scales broad, rigid and brittle, edges finely TOOTHED and rounded at the tip? It is a **black spruce.**

OR

Are the cone scales wedge-shaped with wavy edges?

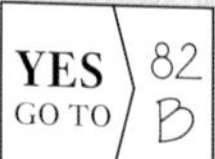

Are the needles somewhat flattened and yellow-green on top? **CLUE:** *The tree is native only along the Pacific coast from northern California to Alaska.* It is a **Sitka spruce.**

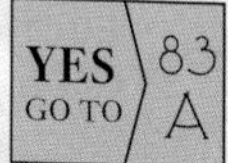

OR

Are the needles 4-sided and blue-green? **CLUE:** *The tree is not a coastal species but is found throughout the western mountains.*

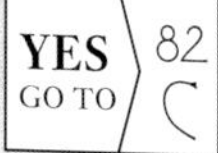

Are the cones 2½–4½" (6.4–11.5 cm) long; the needle tips sharp and bristled? It is a **blue spruce (Colorado blue spruce).**

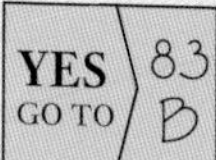

OR

Are the cones 1–2½" (2.5–6.4 cm) long; the needle tips somewhat blunt? It is an **Engelmann spruce.**

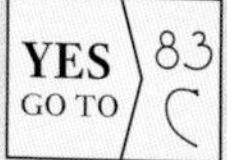

Are the needle bases narrowed so the needle appears stalked; cones hang down; buds pointed? It is a **Douglasfir.**

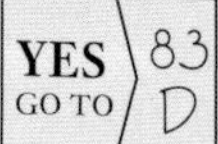

OR

Are the needle bases not stalked; the cones erect with scales that fall off when mature; buds rounded? These are true firs.

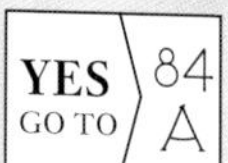

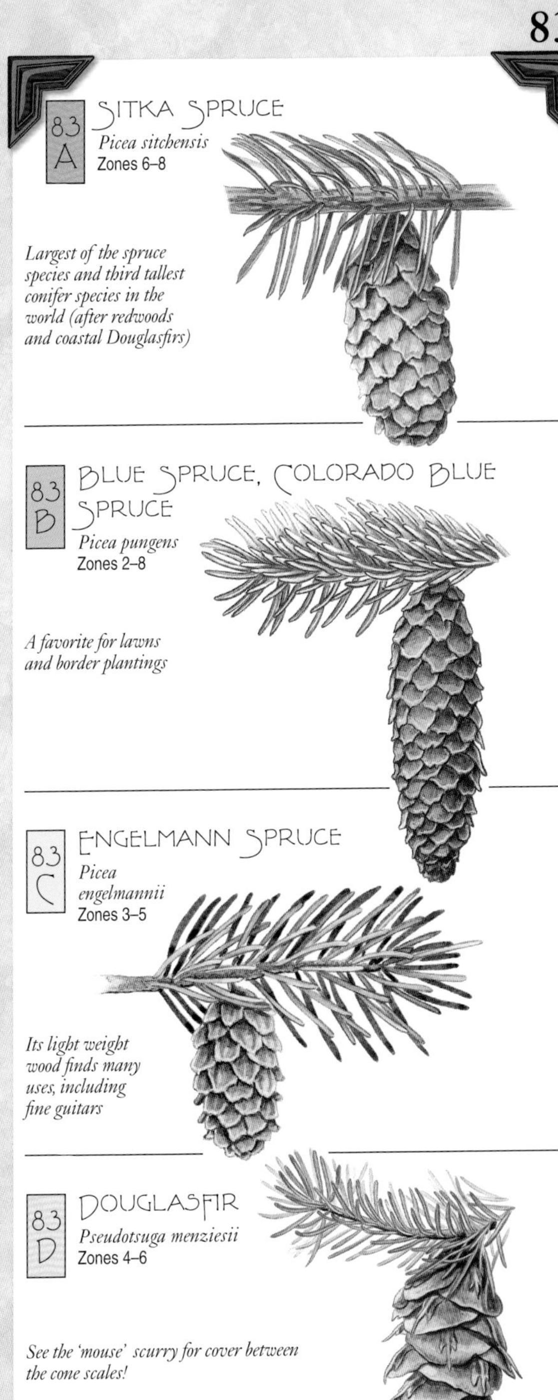

83 A

SITKA SPRUCE

Picea sitchensis
Zones 6–8

Largest of the spruce species and third tallest conifer species in the world (after redwoods and coastal Douglasfirs)

83 B

BLUE SPRUCE, COLORADO BLUE SPRUCE

Picea pungens
Zones 2–8

A favorite for lawns and border plantings

83 C

ENGELMANN SPRUCE

Picea engelmannii
Zones 3–5

Its light weight wood finds many uses, including fine guitars

83 D

DOUGLASFIR

Pseudotsuga menziesii
Zones 4–6

See the 'mouse' scurry for cover between the cone scales!

Are the needles 4-sided; the cones 4–9" (10.2–22.9 cm) long?

OR

Are the needles flattened; the cones 2½–6" (6.4–15.2 cm) long?

YES GO TO 84 C

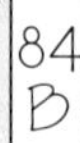

Are the cones about 4–6" (10.2–15.2 cm) long with a fork-like BRACT sticking out under each scale? **CLUE:** *The tree is native from Washington to the northern edge of California.* It is a **noble fir.**

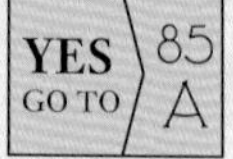

OR

Are the cones about 6–9" (15.2–22.9 cm) long with BRACTS not sticking out from under scales? **CLUE:** *The tree is native from east-central California to southern Oregon.* It is a **California red fir (red fir).**

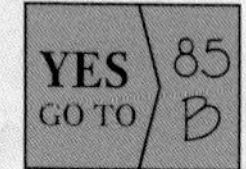

Are the needles 2–3" (5.1–7.6 cm) long and silver-green to silver-blue? It is a **white fir.**

OR

Are the needles 2" (5.1 cm) long or less and darker green, sometimes with 2 white bands on the lower surface?

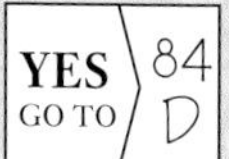

Are the needles blue-green and uniform in color on top and bottom? **CLUE:** *The tree is native throughout the mountains of the West.* It is a **subalpine fir.**

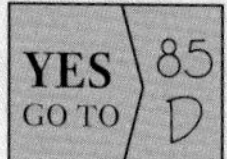

OR

Are the needles dark green and glossy on top with 2 white bands below?

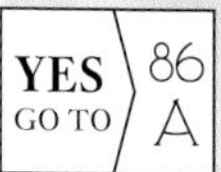

85 A

NOBLE FIR

Abies procera
Zones 5–7

An impressive true fir of the Cascade and Coastal Ranges of the Northwest

85 B

CALIFORNIA RED FIR, RED FIR

Abies magnifica
Zones 5–9

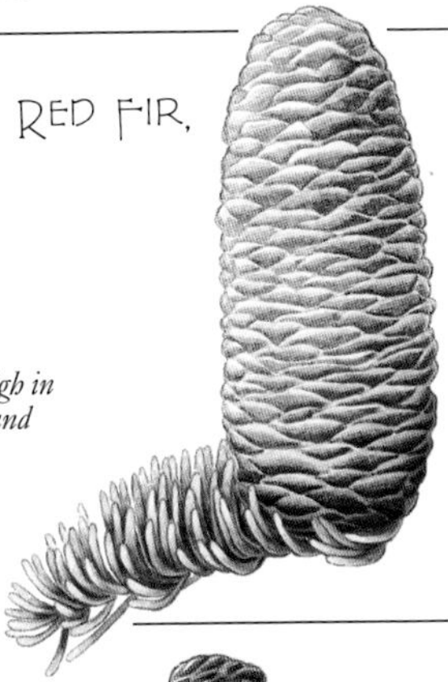

Guardian of water sources high in the mountains of California and southern Oregon

85 C

WHITE FIR

Abies concolor
Zones 4–7

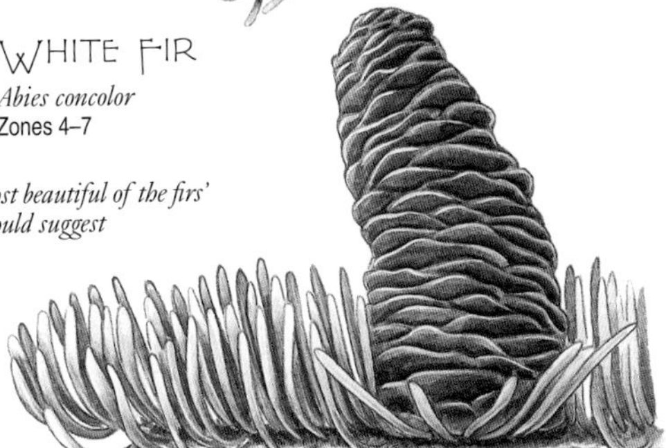

'The most beautiful of the firs' some would suggest

85 D

SUBALPINE FIR

Abies lasiocarpa
Zones 2–6

Narrow and aromatic – the very symbol of Rocky Mountain high country

86

86 A

Are the needles flattened along either side of the twig; the cones 2–4½" (5.1–11.5 cm) long? **CLUE:** *The tree is native from western Montana to British Columbia south to California.* It is a **grand fir.**

YES GO TO 87 A

OR

Are the needles crowded along the upper side of the twig and the cones 3½–6" (8.9–15.2 cm) long? **CLUE:** *The tree is native along the west coast from northern California to Alaska.* It is a **Pacific silver fir.**

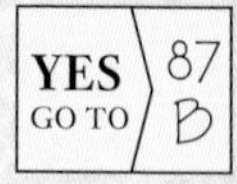

---

86 B

Are the leaves ½–1" (1.3–2.5 cm) long; fruit ⅓" (0.83 cm) long, consisting of a seed partially surrounded by a fleshy red to purple coat? **CLUE:** *Fruit matures in 1 season.* It is a **Pacific yew.**

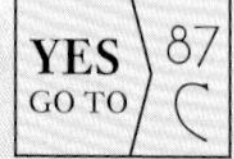

OR

Are the leaves 1–3½" (2.5–8.9 cm) long; fruit 1–1½" (2.5–3.8 cm) long, consisting of a seed entirely covered by a fleshy green to purple coat? **CLUE:** *Fruit matures in 2 seasons.* It is a **California torreya (California nutmeg).**

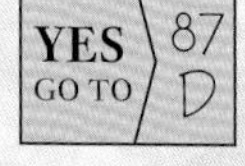

Does the plant have few scale-like leaves or no leaves, just thick fleshy green branches and stems that are ribbed and covered with spines? The fruit is a large red berry. **CLUE:** *The plant is a cactus.* It is a **saguaro.**

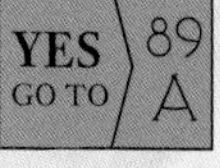

OR

Does the tree have many leaves that are scale-like or awl-shaped? Fruit not as above.

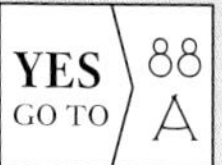

GRAND FIR

Abies grandis
Zones 5–9

A popular Christmas tree with needles in flat planes on its branches

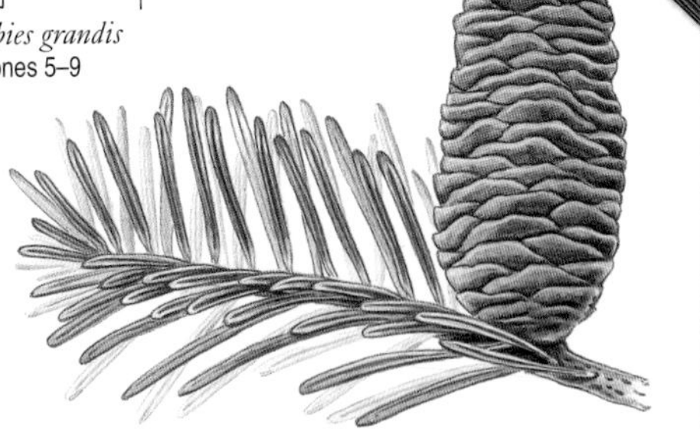

PACIFIC SILVER FIR

Abies amabilis
Zones 5–9

This fir loves rain! It is found in the moistest parts of south-eastern Alaska into the Pacific Northwest

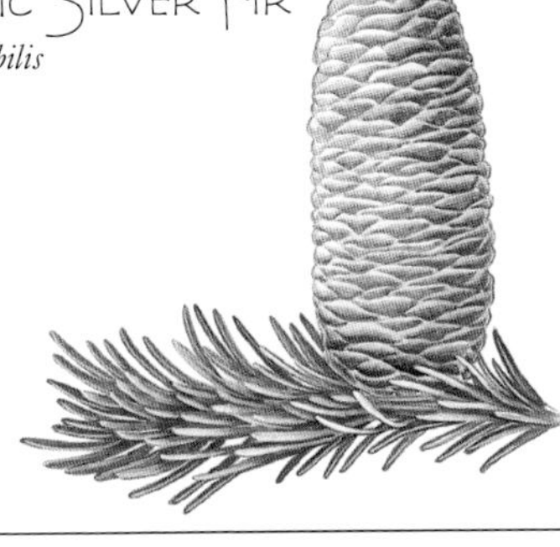

PACIFIC YEW

Taxus brevifolia
Zones 4–9

A gift of life comes to cancer victims through an extract from this tree

CALIFORNIA TORREYA, CALIFORNIA NUTMEG

Torreya californica
Zones 6–9

This yew-like tree is native to the Sierras and Central California

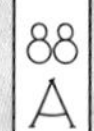

Are the leaves 1/16" (0.16 cm) long, scale-like; clusters of small, showy, pink-petalled flowers; fruit a small CAPSULE containing many tiny, fluffy seeds? This tree is not green year-round. It is a **tamarisk (saltcedar).**

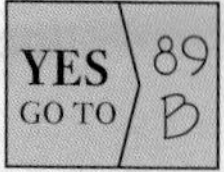

OR

Does the tree bear cones that are sometimes berry-like, and have leaves that hug the twig and are scale-like or awl-shaped? **CLUE:** *These trees are CONIFERS (cone-bearing) and most are EVERGREEN.*

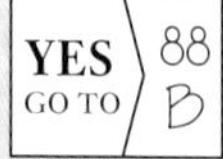

Is the fruit a 2–3½" (5.1–8.9 cm) long woody cone with shield-shaped scales? **CLUE:** *The tree is only native to a few groves in California's Sierra Nevada.* These trees are often very large. It is a **giant sequoia.**

OR

Is the fruit berry-like or a woody cone less than 1½" (3.8 cm) long?

Is the fruit berry-like, often with a whitish, waxy covering? These are juniper trees.

OR

Is the fruit a cone with scales?

Is the bark on the trunk in thick, square plates; the fruit red-brown, ½" (1.3 cm) in diameter? **CLUE:** *The fruit matures in 2 years.* It is an **alligator juniper.**

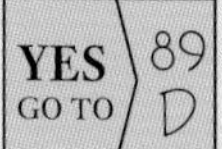

OR

Is the bark on the trunk fibrous and shreddy?

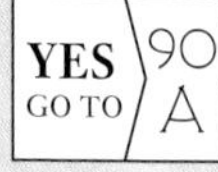

89 A SAGUARO

Carnegiea gigantea
Zone 9

Magnificent symbol of the Southwest desert

89 B TAMARISK, SALTCEDAR

Tamarix chinensis
Zones 4–9

A native of Eurasia and Africa and now an aggressive invasive, especially along watercourses throughout western North America

Potentially Invasive
See page 141

89 C GIANT SEQUOIA

Sequoiadendron giganteum
Zones 6–8

In terms of wood volume, the world's largest tree

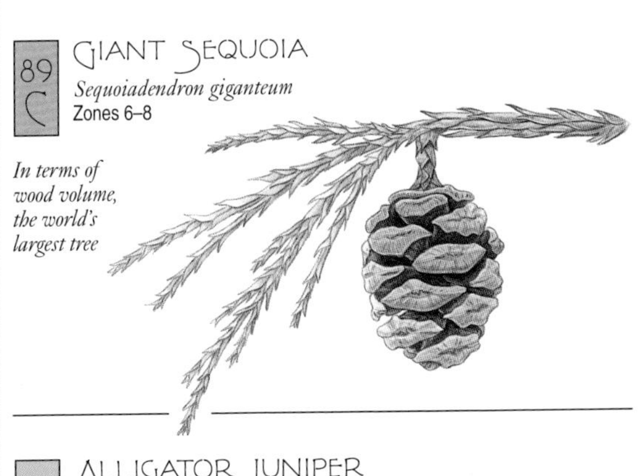

89 D ALLIGATOR JUNIPER

Juniperus deppeana
Zones 6–9

Unmistakable bark gives this large juniper its name

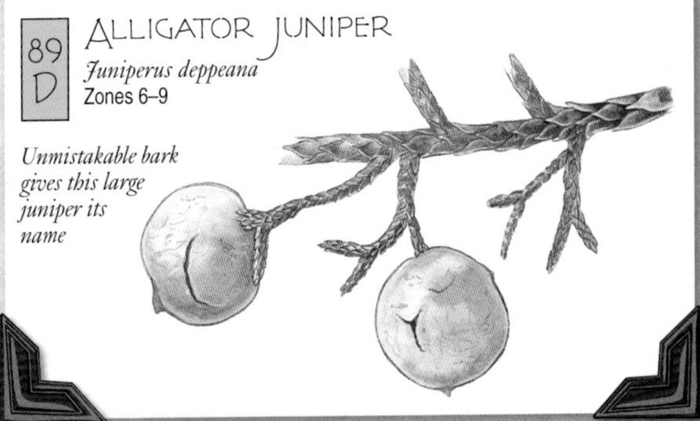

Is the bark reddish brown?

OR

Is the bark grey?

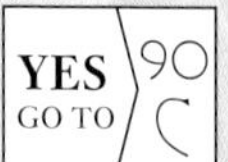

Does the fruit mature in 1 year; is the foliage dark green to purple-green? **CLUE:** *The tree is native to the East, and West to the western Great Plains, though it is widely planted in windbreaks in parts of the west.* It is an **eastern redcedar.**

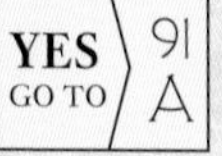

OR

Does the fruit mature in 2 years; is the foliage similar to eastern redcedar but more blue-green? **CLUE:** *The tree is native throughout much of the West.* It is a **Rocky Mountain juniper**.

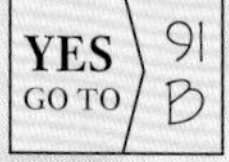

Is the fruit ⅛–¼" (0.125–0.6 cm) in diameter, maturing in 1 year; the foliage gray-green? **CLUE:** *The tree is native to the Southwest and Mexico.* It is a **one-seed juniper.**

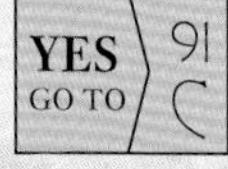

OR

Is the fruit ¼–¾" (0.6–1.9 cm) in diameter, maturing in 2 years; the foliage light yellow-green? **CLUE:** *The tree is native to the inland West south to central Arizona.* It is a **Utah juniper.**

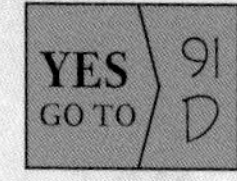

Are the cones oblong with thin scales that are not shield-shaped; the foliage and twigs flattened?

OR

Are the cones round with shield-shaped scales?

91 A

Eastern Redcedar

Juniperus virginiana
Zones 2–9

A juniper, not a true cedar, and the most widely-distributed native conifer in the eastern United States

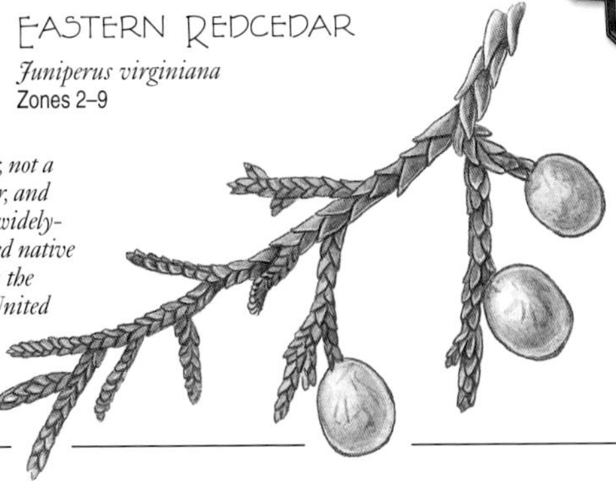

91 B

Rocky Mountain Juniper

Juniperus scopulorum
Zones 3–7

Called 'the most stress-tolerant species available' for windbreaks and other conservation uses

91 C

One-Seed Juniper

Juniperus monosperma
Zones 4–9

Not surprisingly, each cone of this ball-shaped shrub has only one seed

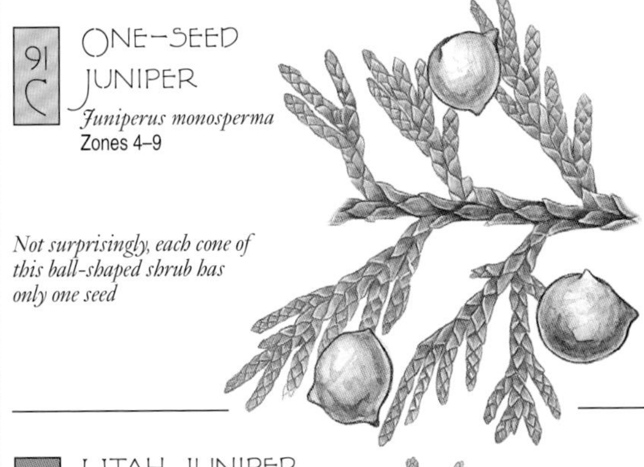

91 D

Utah Juniper

Juniperus osteosperma
Zones 4–7

The most common and widely distributed juniper in the Intermountain West

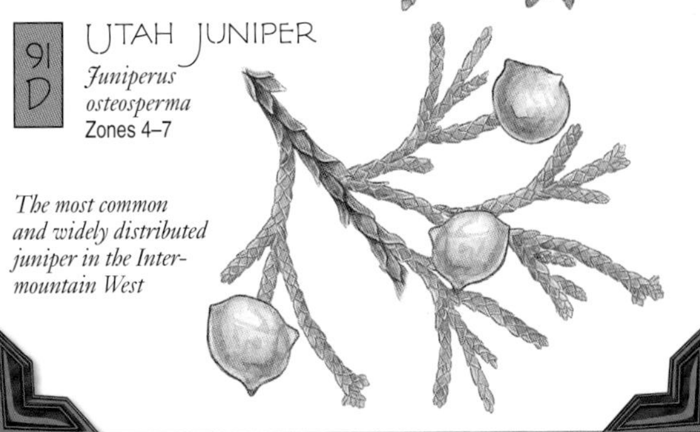

Is the cone ¾–1½" (1.9–3.8 cm) long with 6 leathery scales and does it hang down? It is an **incense-cedar.**

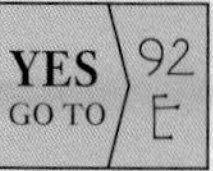

OR

Is the cone generally erect, ⅓–½" (0.8–1.3 cm) long with 6–12 leathery to woody scales? It is a **western redcedar.**

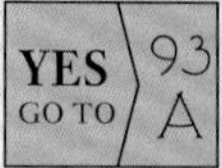

---

92 B

Are the foliage and twigs 4-angled or rounded in cross-section; the cones woody and ¾–1½" (1.9–3.8 cm) in diameter?

YES GO TO 92 C

OR

Are the foliage and twigs flattened in cross-section; the cones leathery to woody and ¼–½" (0.6–1.3 cm) in diameter?

YES GO TO 92 D

---

92 C

Is the foliage light blue to silver-green; the cone ¾–1" (1.9–2.5 cm) in diameter? **CLUE:** *The tree is native from Arizona to southwest Texas and Mexico.* It is an **Arizona cypress.**

YES GO TO 93 B

OR

Is the foliage green to dark green; the cone ⅞–1½" (2.2–3.8 cm) in diameter? **CLUE:** *Tree is native to California.* It is a **Monterey cypress.**

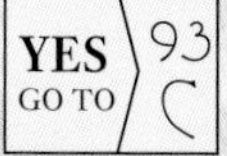

---

92 D

Are flattened groups of twigs arranged horizontally; the leaves 1/16" (0.16 cm) long; the cones ⅓" (0.8 cm) in diameter? **CLUE:** *The tree is native only to northern California and southern Oregon.* It is a **Port Orford-cedar.**

YES GO TO 93 D

OR

Do the flattened groups of twigs droop; are the leaves ⅛" (0.125 cm) long; the cones ¼–½" (0.6–1.3 cm) in diameter? **CLUE:** *Tree is native from Oregon to Alaska.* It is an **Alaska-cedar (yellow-cedar).**

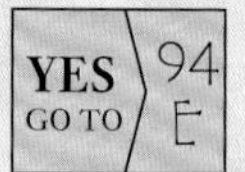

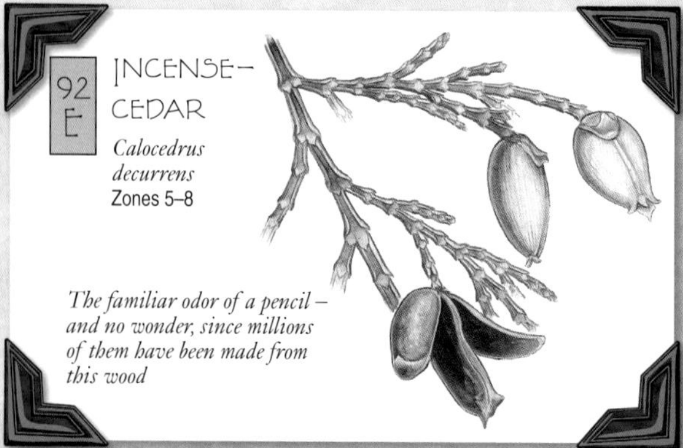

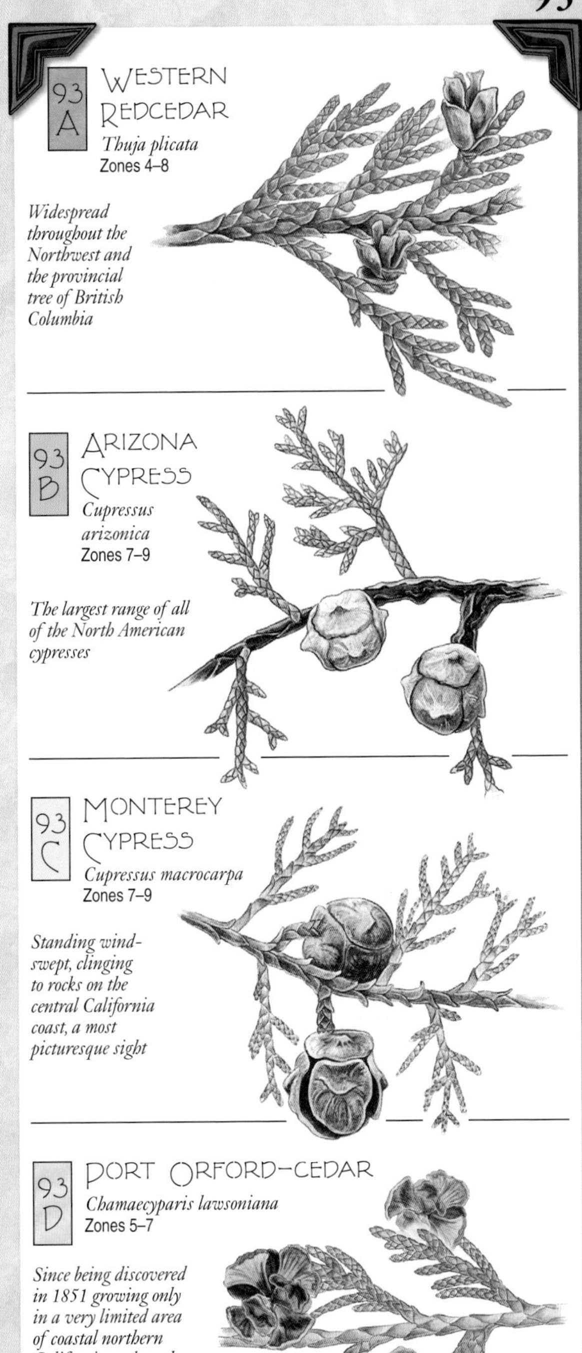

93 A

Western Redcedar

Thuja plicata
Zones 4–8

Widespread throughout the Northwest and the provincial tree of British Columbia

93 B

Arizona Cypress

Cupressus arizonica
Zones 7–9

The largest range of all of the North American cypresses

93 C

Monterey Cypress

Cupressus macrocarpa
Zones 7–9

Standing windswept, clinging to rocks on the central California coast, a most picturesque sight

93 D

Port Orford-Cedar

Chamaecyparis lawsoniana
Zones 5–7

Since being discovered in 1851 growing only in a very limited area of coastal northern California and southern Oregon, this beautiful tree has been marketed worldwide for use in landscaping.

94 A

Are the leaves OPPOSITE in groups of 2–3, ENTIRE heart-shaped or with very narrow BLADES 5–15" (12.7–38.1 cm) long? **CLUE:** *The fruit is a 7–12" (17.8–30.5 cm) long slender CAPSULE.*

YES GO TO 94 B

OR

Are the leaves ENTIRE, BLADES less than 6" (15.2 cm) long, with veins that curve to follow the leaf edge? **CLUE:** *The fruit is a berry-like DRUPE.* These are dogwood trees.

YES GO TO 94 C

OR

LOBE

Are the leaves PALMATELY LOBED (like fingers on the palm of a hand)? **CLUE:** *The fruit is a SAMARA in pairs.* These are maple trees.

YES GO TO 94 D

94 B

Are the leaves heart-shaped and 8–12" (20.3–30.5 cm) long? **CLUE:** *The tree is not native in the West.* It is a **northern catalpa.**

YES GO TO 95 A

OR

Are the leaves 5–12" (12.7–30.5 cm) long, very narrow, and linear? **CLUE:** *The tree is native only to the extreme Southwest.* It is a **desert-willow.**

YES GO TO 95 B

94 C

Are the leaves 3–5" (7.6–12.7 cm) long; the fruit bright orange-red; the flowers often surrounded by large, white, petal-like BRACTS? It is a **Pacific dogwood.**

YES GO TO 95 C

OR

Are the leaves 1–3" (2.5–7.6 cm) long; the fruit (DRUPE) white to light blue, the flowers not surrounded by BRACTS? It is a **brown dogwood.**

YES GO TO 95 D

94 D

Do the LOBED leaves have sharply TOOTHED edges with sharp-angled SINUSES?

YES GO TO 96 A

OR

SINUS

Do the leaves have LOBES that are ENTIRE or have a few rounded TEETH and rounded SINUSES?

YES GO TO 96 D

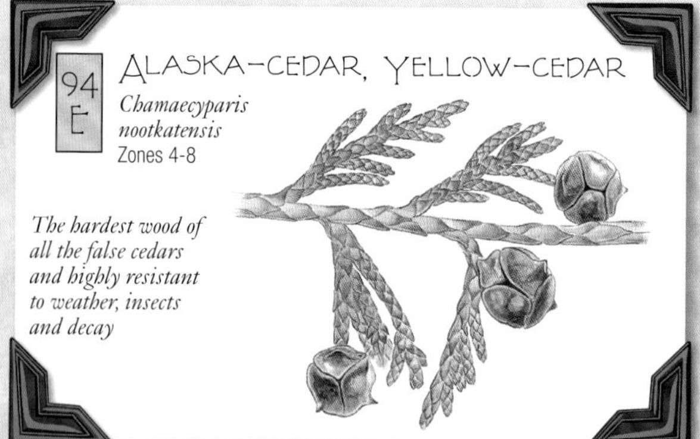

Northern Catalpa

Catalpa speciosa
Zones 4-9

The cigar tree - nicknamed for its slender seedpods that turn brown - has huge elephant ear leaves

Desert-Willow

Chilopsis linearis
Zones 7-9

The flowers are gorgeous trumpets, especially attractive to hummingbirds

Pacific Dogwood

Cornus nuttallii
Zones 7-9

The provincial flower of British Columbia

Brown Dogwood

Cornus glabrata
Zones 7-9

Usually found on the banks of waterways in its native California and Oregon

96

96 A Is this a shrub or small tree? — **YES** GO TO 96 B

OR

Is this a medium to large tree when mature? **CLUE:** *This tree is not native to the West.* — **YES** GO TO 96 C

---

96 B Do the leaves have a middle LOBE equal to, or only slightly longer than, the side LOBES? **CLUE:** *This tree is native throughout the West.* It is a **Rocky Mountain maple.** — **YES** GO TO 96 E

OR

Do the leaves have a middle LOBE much longer than the side LOBES? **CLUE:** *This tree is not native to the West.* It is an **Amur maple (ginnala maple).** — **YES** GO TO 97 A

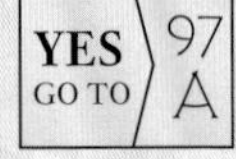

96 C Are the leaves about 4" (10.2 cm) across, mostly 3-LOBED (some 5), with the SAMARA (winged fruit) about ¾" (1.9 cm) long? It is a **red maple.** — **YES** GO TO 97 B

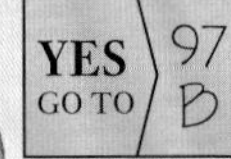

SAMARA

OR

Are the leaves about 6" (15.2 cm) across, deeply 5-LOBED, with the SAMARA about 2" (5.1 cm) long? It is a **silver maple.** — **YES** GO TO 97 C

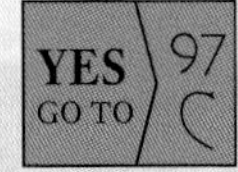

---

96 D Are the leaves 8–12" (20.3–30.5 cm) long? **CLUE:** *This tree is native or planted along the Pacific coast.* It is a **bigleaf maple.** — **YES** GO TO 97 D

OR

Are the leaves 2–5" (5.1–12.7 cm) long? **CLUE:** *This tree is native in scattered areas of the inland West.* It is a **bigtooth maple (canyon maple).** — **YES** GO TO 98 E

97 A
AMUR MAPLE, GINNALA MAPLE
Acer ginnala
Zones 3–8
Potentially Invasive
See page 141
A choice patio tree with early leaves, pretty white flowers, and gorgeous red fall colors
97 B
RED MAPLE
Acer rubrum
Zones 3–9
A part of the tree is red in all seasons, making it one of nature's best named trees
97 C
SILVER MAPLE
Acer saccharinum
Zones 3–9
See its leaves shimmer like silver and watch its super fast annual growth – even in tough urban soil
97 D
BIGLEAF MAPLE
Acer macrophyllum
Zones 5–9
Leaves shaped like a giant's hand, often 12 inches across

Are the COMPOUND leaves PALMATE (leaf BLADES on one leaf-stem arranged like fingers on a hand); the fruit a 3-part leathery CAPSULE with smooth, hard, nut-like seeds inside?

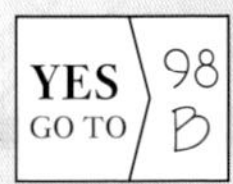

OR

Are the COMPOUND leaves PINNATE (leaf BLADES arranged like the vanes of a feather); the fruit a single or double SAMARA or a berry?

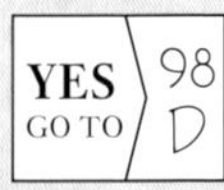

---

98 B

Do the leaves usually have 7 BLADES; are the buds normally gummy?
CLUE: *This tree is not native to the West.* It is a **horsechestnut.**

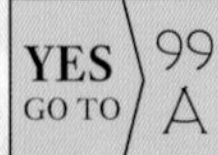

OR

Do the leaves usually have 5 BLADES; are the buds not gummy?

Is the outside of the fruit prickly?
CLUE: *This tree is not native to the West.* It is an **Ohio buckeye.**

YES GO TO 99 B

OR

Is the outside of the fruit not prickly?
CLUE: *This tree is native to California.* It is a **California buckeye.**

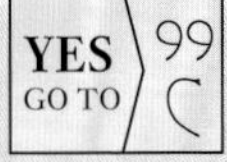

Do the leaves usually have 3–5 LOBED or coarsely TOOTHED blades; the fruit is a double SAMARA; twigs green to purplish-green? It is a **boxelder (ashleaf maple).**

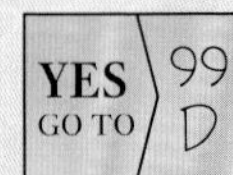

OR

Do the leaves usually have 3–13 non-LOBED blades; is the fruit a single SAMARA or a berry?

99 A

HORSECHESTNUT

Aesculus hippocastanum
Zones 4-7

Large white flowers held aloft like torches in the spring yield shiny buckeyes by fall

99 B

OHIO BUCKEYE

Aesculus glabra
Zones 4-7

See what early Indians called the "eye of a buck" in the fruit of this enjoyable tree

99 C

CALIFORNIA BUCKEYE

Aesculus californica
Zones 7-9

Large white flowers brighten the shadier hills of central California when this buckeye bursts into bloom

99 D

BOXELDER, ASHLEAF MAPLE

Acer negundo
Zones 3-9

A maple like no other with its compound leaves

100

Do the COMPOUND leaves have 5–9 BLADES and blue-black, berry-like fruit held in flat-topped bunches? It is a **blue elderberry.**

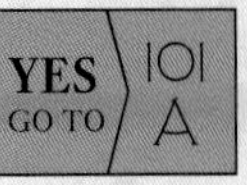

OR

Do the COMPOUND leaves have 5–13 BLADES (occasionally 3); the fruit a single-winged SAMARA? These are ash trees.

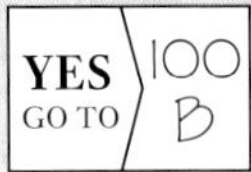

Are the young twigs, leaf stalks, and leaf undersides densely covered with velvety hairs? **CLUE:** *These trees are native to the Pacific coast states, the Southwest, and Mexico.*

OR

Are the young twigs, leaf stalks, and leaf undersides not covered or sparsely covered with velvety hairs? **CLUE:** *These trees are native to the eastern U.S. and Great Plains or High Plains, or to Europe; not the Pacific coast or Southwest.*

Are the COMPOUND leaves 3–6" (7.6–15.2 cm) long with BLADES 1–1½" (2.5–3.8 cm) long? **CLUE:** *This tree is native to the Southwest and Mexico.* It is a **velvet ash.**

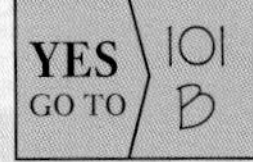

OR

Are the COMPOUND leaves 5–14" (12.7–35.6 cm) long with BLADES 3–7" (7.6–17.8 cm) long? **CLUE:** *This tree is native to the Pacific coast states.* It is an **Oregon ash.**

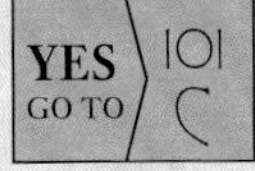

Are the buds black? **CLUE:** *This tree is native to Europe but is sometimes planted in the U.S.* It is a **European ash.**

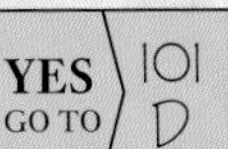

OR

Are the buds brown or red-brown? **CLUE:** *This tree is native from eastern Alberta to Ontario, eastern U.S. and Great Plains.*

101 A
BLUE ELDERBERRY
Sambucus caerulea
Zones 7–9
Fine berries for wine, pies— or the birds
101 B
VELVET ASH
Fraxinus velutina
Zones 7–9
A sure sign of water – above or below ground – in the arid Southwest
101 C
OREGON ASH
Fraxinus latifolia
Zones 7–9
Important to wildlife habitat in its ribbon-like distribution along the streams west of the Cascades and south to central California
101 D
EUROPEAN ASH
Fraxinus excelsior
Zones 3–7
Widespread in Europe where it is a favorite with butterflies

Are the leaf BLADES slightly hairy underneath, with yellow fall color? **CLUE:** *LEAF SCARS nearly straight across the top.* It is a **green ash.**

YES GO TO 103 A

OR

Are the twigs and leaf stalks smooth and glossy? Leaf underside often whitish. Leaves bronze to purple in fall. **CLUE:** *LEAF SCARS deeply notched or U-shaped.* It is a **white ash.**

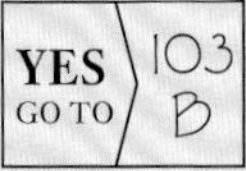

Are the leaves fan-shaped, with veins extending out from the leaf base? Sometimes 1–2 notches form LOBES along the MARGIN. It is a CONIFER known as **ginkgo.**

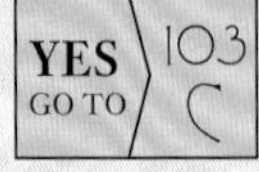

OR

Are the leaves not fan-shaped?

Are most of the leaves LOBED?

YES GO TO 102 D

OR

Are most of the leaves not LOBED?

Are the leaves ⅓–½" (0.8–1.3 cm) long; the small, nut-like fruit has a long, hairy tip? It is a **Mexican cliffrose.**

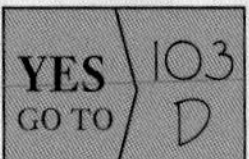

OR

Are the leaves generally more than 1" (2.5 cm) long?

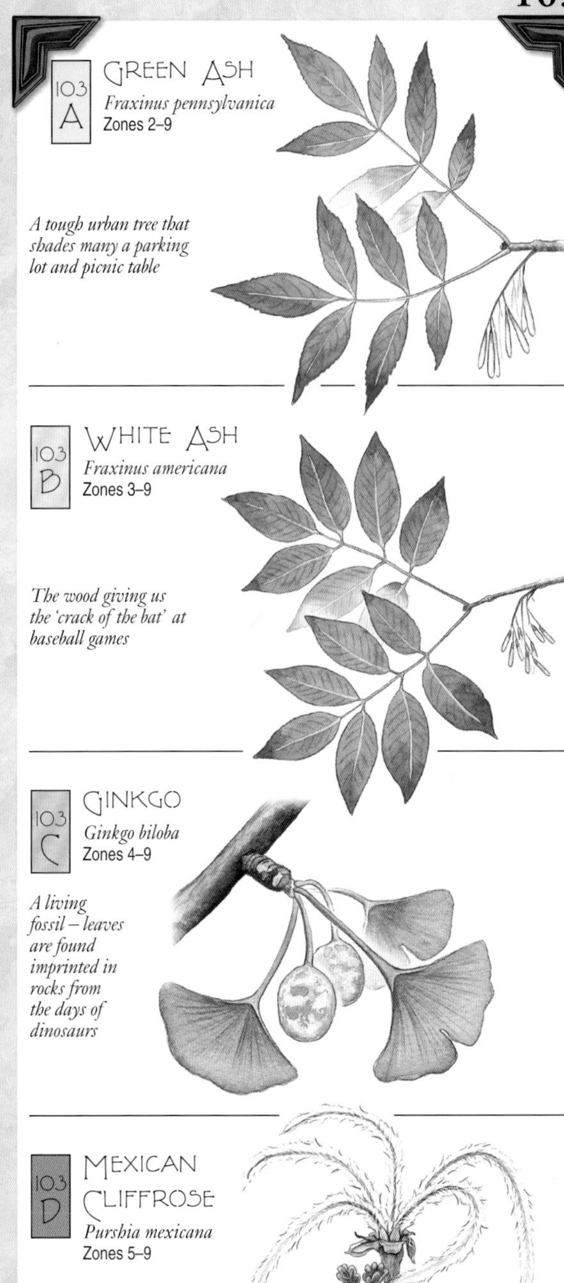

103 A

Green Ash

Fraxinus pennsylvanica
Zones 2–9

A tough urban tree that shades many a parking lot and picnic table

103 B

White Ash

Fraxinus americana
Zones 3–9

The wood giving us the 'crack of the bat' at baseball games

103 C

Ginkgo

Ginkgo biloba
Zones 4–9

A living fossil – leaves are found imprinted in rocks from the days of dinosaurs

103 D

Mexican Cliffrose

Purshia mexicana
Zones 5–9

Long-lasting blooms and plummed seed heads

Are the leaves, when LOBED, PALMATELY LOBED (like fingers on a hand)?

OR

Are the leaves, when LOBED, PINNATELY (like vanes on a feather) or irregularly LOBED?

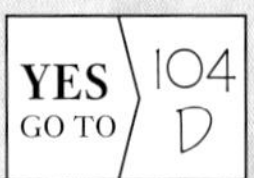

Are the leaves at least 4–10" (10.2–25.4 cm) wide; the PETIOLE base hollow and covering the side buds; the bark of the upper trunk and branches smooth or peeling off in large plates; the fruit a dry ball on a long stalk?

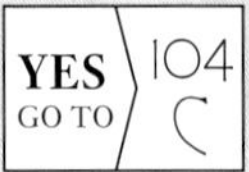

OR

Are the leaves 1–4" (2.5–10.2 cm) wide with undersides and twigs covered with white hair; the PETIOLE base is not hollow and does not cover the side buds? It is a **white poplar.**

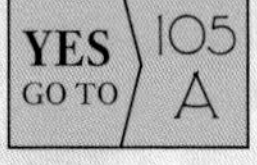

Are the leaves 5–7 LOBED?
CLUE: *This tree is native to Arizona and New Mexico.* It is an **Arizona sycamore.**

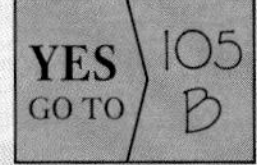

OR

Are the leaves 3–5 LOBED?
CLUE: *This tree is native to California.* It is a **California sycamore.**

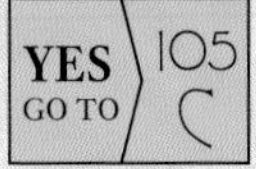

Do the twigs have slender, tapered thorns?

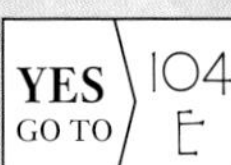

OR

Do the twigs not have slender, tapered thorns?

Is the fruit nearly black and berry-like?
CLUE: *This tree is native throughout the West, Northwest, and parts of Canada.* It is a **black hawthorn.**

OR

Is the fruit red and berry-like?
CLUE: *These trees are native to the eastern and central U.S.*

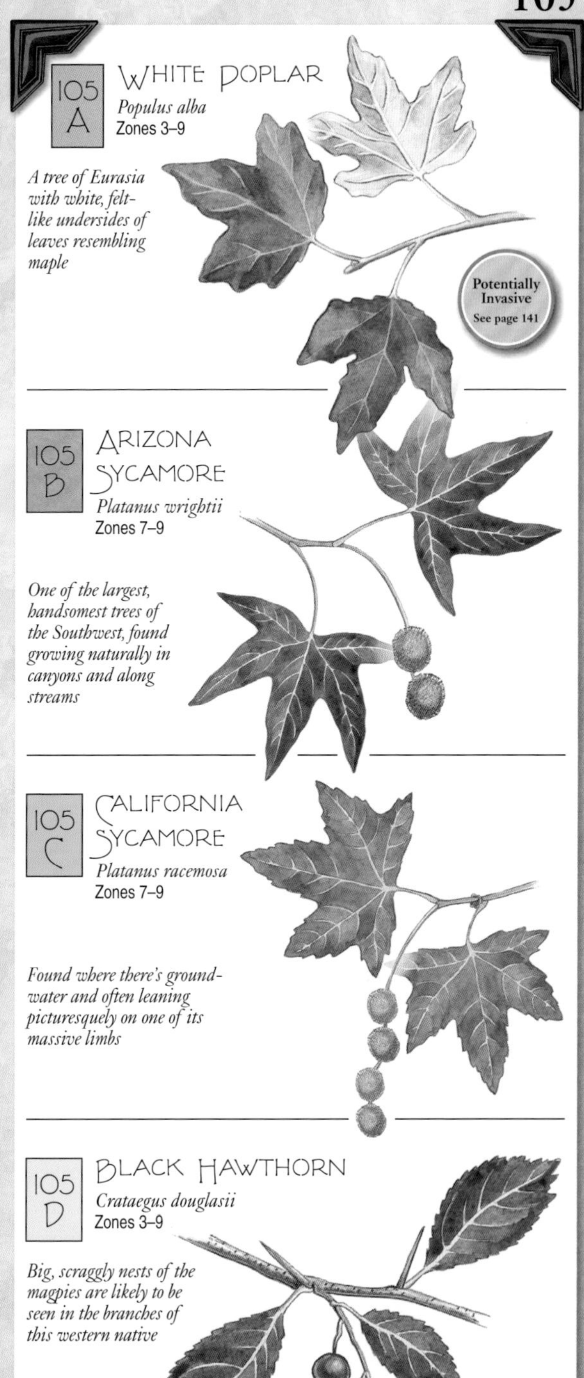

105 A
WHITE POPLAR
Populus alba
Zones 3–9
A tree of Eurasia with white, felt-like undersides of leaves resembling maple
Potentially Invasive
See page 141
105 B
ARIZONA SYCAMORE
Platanus wrightii
Zones 7–9
One of the largest, handsomest trees of the Southwest, found growing naturally in canyons and along streams
105 C
CALIFORNIA SYCAMORE
Platanus racemosa
Zones 7–9
Found where there's ground-water and often leaning picturesquely on one of its massive limbs
105 D
BLACK HAWTHORN
Crataegus douglasii
Zones 3–9
Big, scraggly nests of the magpies are likely to be seen in the branches of this western native

Are the leaves generally LOBED; fruit ¼" (0.6 cm) in diameter? It is a **Washington hawthorn.**

OR

Are the leaves generally LOBED and downy; fruit ½–1" (1.3–2.5 cm) in diameter? It is a **downy hawthorn.**

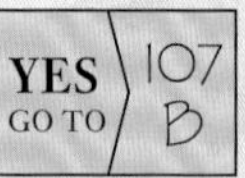

Are the leaves downy and jagged-TOOTHED or slightly LOBED; twigs with short SPURS; fruit a small apple or POME? It is a **crabapple.**

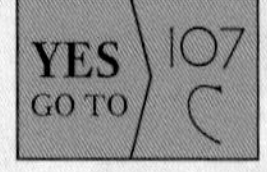

OR

Are the leaves, twigs, and fruit not as above?

Do the leaves have 3 main veins spreading out from near the leaf base to several LOBES (some leaves not LOBED); one bud at the tip of each twig; fleshy fruit?

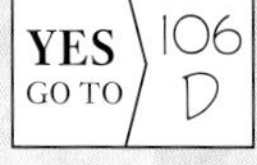

OR

Do the leaves have 1 MIDRIB; several buds clustered at the tips of the twigs; fruits that are acorns? These are oaks.

Are the leaves 1–2" (2.5–5.1 cm) long, rough on top and bottom, and the fruit nearly black when mature? **CLUE:** *This tree is native to the Southwest from Arizona to western Texas and southern Oklahoma.* It is a **Texas mulberry.**

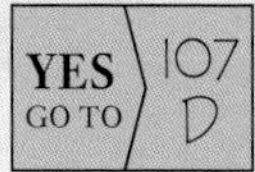

OR

Are the leaves over 2½" (6.4 cm) long and sometimes hairy but not rough on leaf undersurface? Fruit white, pink, or dark purple when mature. **CLUE:** *These trees are native or naturalized in the eastern half of the U.S.*

107 A

WASHINGTON HAWTHORN

Crataegus phaenopyrum
Zones 4–8

Showy white flowers blanket the crown in late spring

107 B

DOWNY HAWTHORN

Crataegus mollis
Zones 3–6

Omaha Indians once steeped the twigs of this tree to make tea

107 C

CRABAPPLE

Malus species
Zones 3–9

With more than 900 varieties, most are identifiable only by experts

107 D

TEXAS MULBERRY

Morus microphylla
Zones 6–9

A small tree of canyons and a delight to birds and wine-makers

Are the leaves rough on top, UNLOBED to 3-LOBED; mature fruit (on female trees) red to dark purple? It is a **red mulberry.**

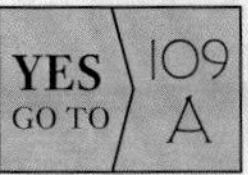

OR

Are the leaves smooth and glossy on top, UNLOBED to many-LOBED; mature fruit (on female trees) white, pink, or purple? It is a **white mulberry.**

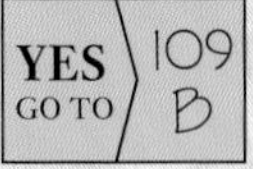

Are the leaf LOBES blunt or rounded? **CLUE:** *The inner surface of the acorn shell, next to the fleshy acorn meat, is not hairy.*

OR

Are the leaf LOBES sharp and bristle tipped? **CLUE:** *The inner surface of the acorn shell is hairy.*

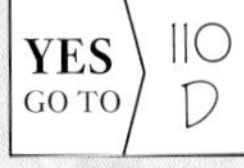

Is the acorn cap bristly or slightly fringed around the rim? **CLUE:** *These trees are native to southern Saskatchewan and New Brunswick, eastern U.S. or Great Plains.*

OR

Is the acorn not as above? **CLUE:** *These trees are native to the western U.S.*

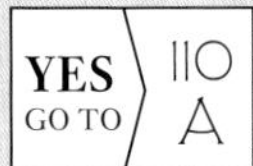

Are the leaves usually deeply LOBED below the middle and shallowly LOBED above; with a bristly acorn cap with little or no stalk that encloses a half or more of the acorn? **CLUE:** *The bark on twigs is often in corky ridges.* It is a **bur oak.**

OR

Are the leaves shallowly LOBED or coarsely TOOTHED; with a slightly fringed acorn cap on a 1–3" (2.5–7.6 cm) stalk that encloses a half or less of the acorn? **CLUE:** *The bark peels on upper branches and twigs.* It is a **swamp white oak.**

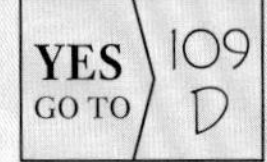

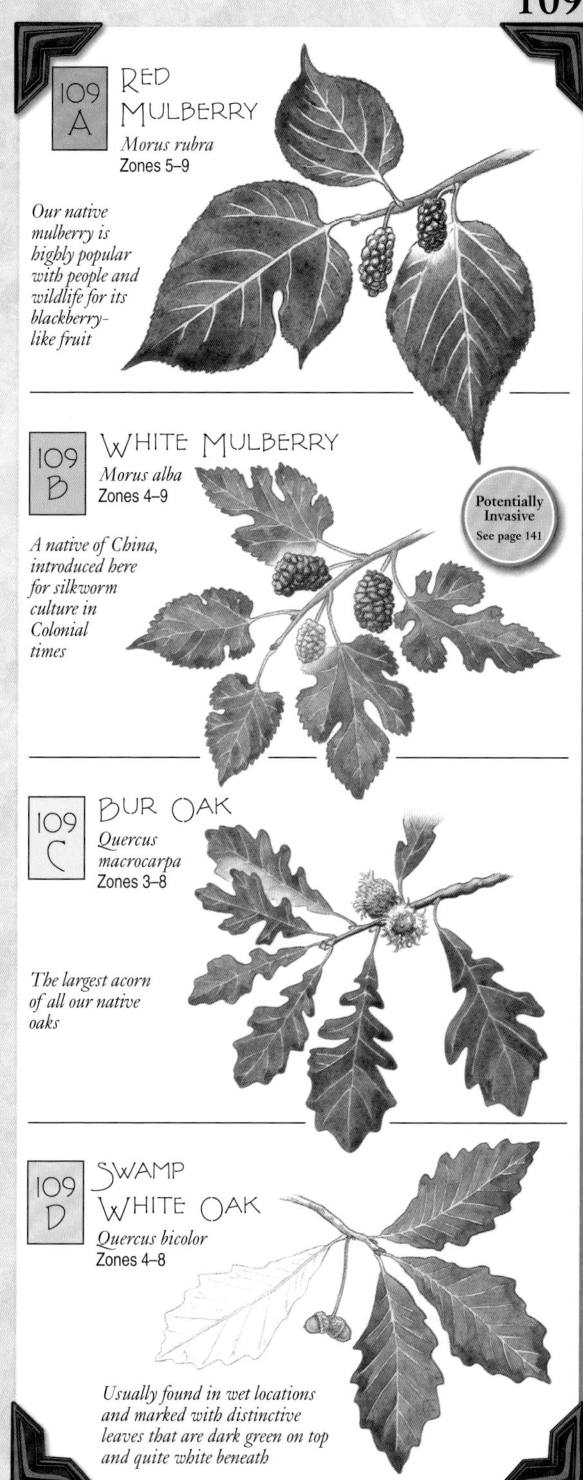

109 A RED MULBERRY

Morus rubra
Zones 5–9

Our native mulberry is highly popular with people and wildlife for its blackberry-like fruit

109 B WHITE MULBERRY

Morus alba
Zones 4–9

Potentially Invasive
See page 141

A native of China, introduced here for silkworm culture in Colonial times

109 C BUR OAK

Quercus macrocarpa
Zones 3–8

The largest acorn of all our native oaks

109 D SWAMP WHITE OAK

Quercus bicolor
Zones 4–8

Usually found in wet locations and marked with distinctive leaves that are dark green on top and quite white beneath

110

Are the leaves dark blue-green and shallowly or irregularly LOBED? It is a **blue oak.**

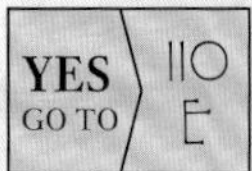

OR

Are the leaves deeply LOBED and not dark blue-green?

---

110 B

Is the acorn less than ¾" (1.9 cm) long and the tree usually shrubby? **CLUE:** *This tree is native to the interior West, not coastal states.* It is a **Gambel oak.**

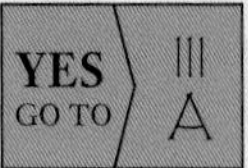

OR

Is the acorn ¾" (1.9 cm) long or more and the tree not shrubby? **CLUE:** *These trees are native to the Pacific coastal states.*

---

110 C

Are the leaves 2½–3" (6.4–7.6 cm) long; and the acorns 1–2¼" (2.5–5.6 cm) long and slender? **CLUE:** *This tree is native only to California.* It is a **valley oak.**

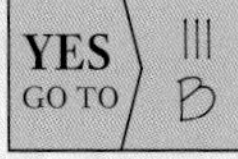

OR

Are the leaves over 3" (7.6 cm) long; the acorns 1–1¼" (2.5–3.2 cm) long and not slender? **CLUE:** *This tree is native to California, Oregon, Washington and British Columbia.* It is an **Oregon white oak.**

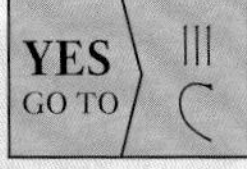

---

110 D

Are the leaves 5–7 LOBED and usually hairy, with 1–1½" (2.5–3.8 cm) long acorns with a cap enclosing ⅓–¾ (.84–1.9 cm) of their length? **CLUE:** *This tree is native to California and Oregon.* It is a **California black oak.**

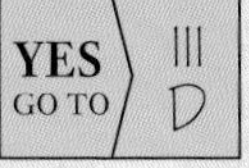

OR

Are the leaves 7–11 LOBED and smooth; with ¾–1" (1.9–2.5 cm) long acorns enclosed in a shallow cap? **CLUE:** *This tree is native to parts of eastern Canada and the eastern U.S.* It is a **northern red oak.**

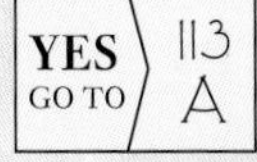

III A

Gambel Oak

Quercus gambelii
Zones 4–8

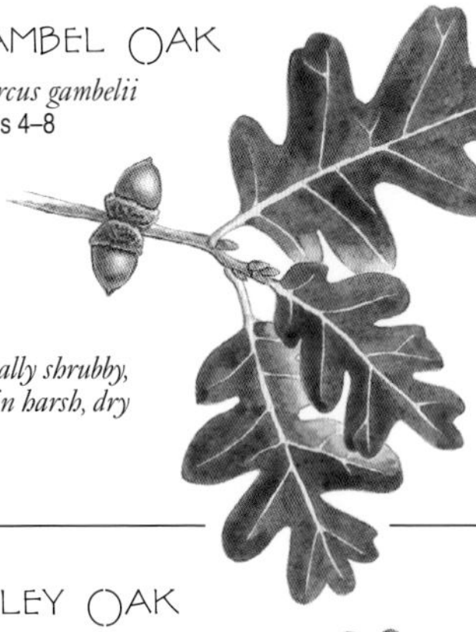

Common and usually shrubby, it's able to thrive in harsh, dry conditions

III B

Valley Oak

Quercus lobata
Zones 9–10

"For about 20 miles it could only compare to a park…"

—George Vancouver, 1796, viewing these trees while exploring the Santa Clara Valley

III C

Oregon White Oak

Quercus garryana
Zones 7–9

The only native oak in British Columbia and Washington and the principal one in Oregon

III D

California Black Oak

Quercus kelloggii
Zones 6–9

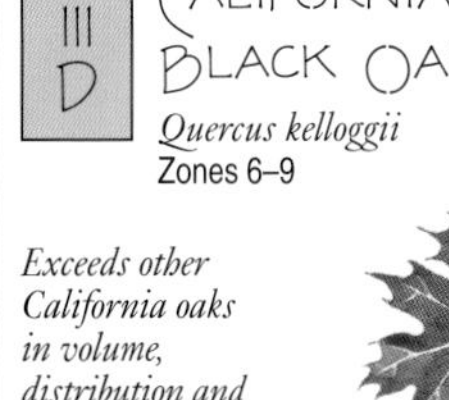

Exceeds other California oaks in volume, distribution and altitudinal range

112 A

Is the fruit an acorn; the leaves PERSISTENT (DECIDUOUS leaf BLADES that remain on the tree for more than one year)? **YES** GO TO 112 B

OR

Is the fruit not an acorn; the leaves either PERSISTENT or DECIDUOUS? **YES** GO TO 116 A

---

112 B

Do the leaves PERSIST on the tree for 3–4 years? **YES** GO TO 112 C

OR

Do the leaves PERSIST on the tree for 2 years or less? **YES** GO TO 112 D

---

112 C

Is the acorn cap spiny, the acorn ¾–1" (1.9–2.5 cm) long? **CLUE:** *The shiny stiff green leaves may be wavy-TOOTHED or UNTOOTHED.* It is a **tanoak.** **YES** GO TO 113 B

OR

Is the acorn cap scaly, the acorn ½–2" (1.3–5.1 cm) long? **CLUE:** *Some of the leathery leaves have prickly holly-like MARGINS.* It is a **canyon live oak.** **YES** GO TO 113 C

---

112 D

Are the trees found in the Southwest along the Mexican border? **YES** GO TO 112 E

OR

Are the trees found mainly in California and sometimes also north along the coast? **YES** GO TO 114 C

Is the acorn shell woolly on the inside next to the nut meat? It is an **Emory oak.** **YES** GO TO 113 D

OR

Is the acorn shell smooth on the inside near the nut meat? **YES** GO TO 114 A

113 A
NORTHERN RED OAK
Quercus rubra
Zones 3–8
Strong and durable, a fine selection to shade streets and playgrounds
113 B
TANOAK
Lithocarpus densiflorus
Zones 7–9
With flowers like a chestnut and acorns like an oak, this unusual broadleaf evergreen reaches maximum growth in the coastal ranges of California.
113 C
CANYON LIVE OAK
Quercus chrysolepis
Zones 7–9
Like other live oaks, its leathery leaves are 'evergreen'
113 D
EMORY OAK
Quercus emoryi
Zones 7–9
Sweet, edible acorns are produced annually

114

Are the leaves ½–1¼" (1.3–3.2 cm) long with many sharp TEETH? **CLUE:** *The acorns shaped "like little tops" are the namesake of this tree.* It is a **turbinella oak.**

YES GO TO 114 E

OR

Are the leaves 1–4" (2.5–10.2 cm) long with no TEETH or a few short, rounded TEETH?

YES GO TO 114 B

Are the leaves smooth on the bottom, 1–2" (2.5–5.1 cm) long; acorns are ½–¾" (1.3–1.9 cm) long? It is a **Mexican blue oak.**

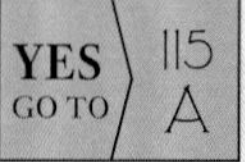

OR

Are the leaves hairy on the bottom, 1–4" (2.5–10.2 cm) long; acorns are ¾–1" (1.9–2.5 cm) long? It is an **Arizona white oak.**

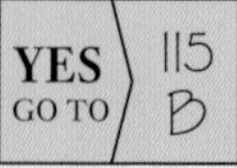

Is the acorn shell smooth on the inside next to the nut meat? **CLUE:** *The acorn matures in one year.* It is an **Engelmann oak.**

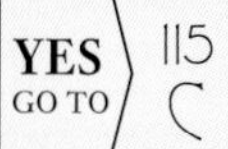

OR

Is the acorn shell woolly on the inside near the nut meat?

Are the acorns somewhat slender and more than half covered by a thin cap? **CLUE:** *The acorn matures in two years.* It is an **interior live oak.**

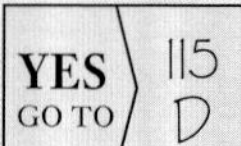

OR

Are the acorns very slender, cone-shaped, and less than half covered by a thin cap? **CLUE:** *The acorn matures in one year.* It is a **coast live oak (California live oak).**

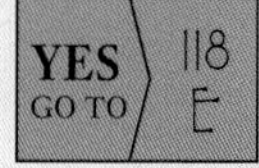

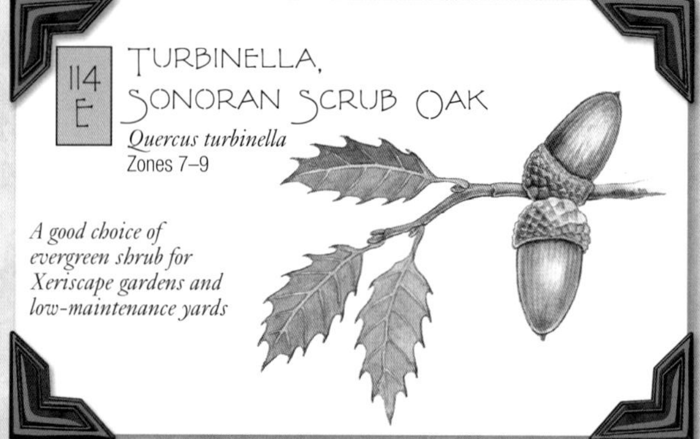

115 A

MEXICAN BLUE OAK

Quercus oblongifolia
Zones 7–9

Bluish color is evident on the small, oblong leaves

115 B

ARIZONA WHITE OAK

Quercus arizonica
Zones 7–9

Growing naturally in Arizona and New Mexico, its leaves look more like beech than most oaks even though all are members of the Beech Family

115 C

ENGELMANN OAK

Quercus engelmannii
Zones 8–9

A spectacular oak found growing naturally only from near Pasadena, California to northern Mexico

115 D

INTERIOR LIVE OAK

Quercus wislizenii
Zones 8–9

Found on the drier slopes of California's coastal mountains

Are the leaf MARGINS sometimes ENTIRE and sometimes very finely TOOTHED; the fruit a cherry? **CLUE:** *Native to California, leaves are PERSISTENT.* It is a **Catalina cherry.**

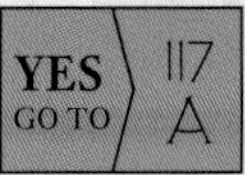

OR

Are the leaf MARGINS always ENTIRE?

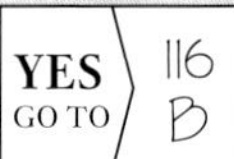

OR

Are the leaf MARGINS always TOOTHED?

Are the leaves DECIDUOUS?

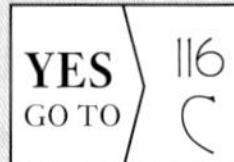

OR

Are the leaves PERSISTENT or EVERGREEN?

Are the leaves, young twigs, and small, olive-like fruit covered with silvery scales; with thorns often present? It is a **Russian-olive.**

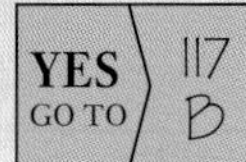

OR

Are the leaves, twigs, and fruit not covered with silvery scales?

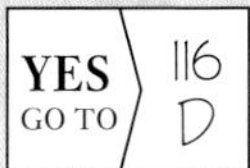

Are the heart-shaped leaves wider than they are long, with fruit a small pod (LEGUME)? **CLUE:** *Spring blooms purple to red, native to the Southwest.* It is a **California redbud (western redbud)**.

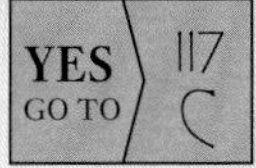

OR

Are the leaves longer than they are wide, the fruit a dry, orange to yellow DRUPE. **CLUE:** *This tree is native from the southern Great Plains west to California, Oregon, and Washington.* It is a **netleaf hackberry.**

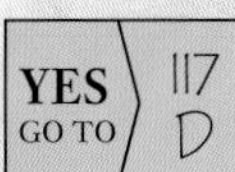

OR

Are the leaves 5–12" (12.7–30.5 cm) long, very narrow and sometimes arranged OPPOSITELY; fruit a 4–8" (10.2–20.3 cm) long, narrow, beanlike CAPSULE? **CLUE:** *The tree is native only to the extreme Southwest.* It is a **desert-willow.**

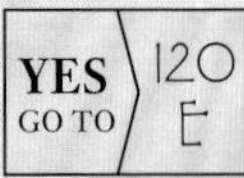

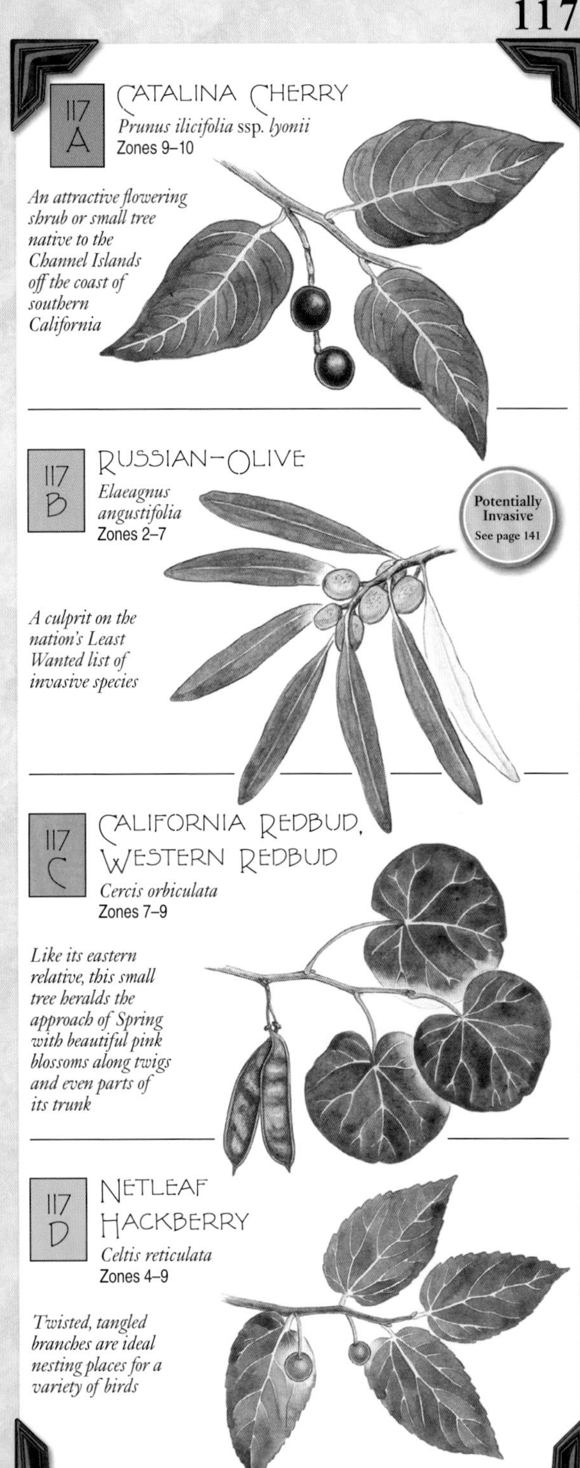
117 A
CATALINA CHERRY
Prunus ilicifolia ssp. lyonii
Zones 9–10
An attractive flowering shrub or small tree native to the Channel Islands off the coast of southern California
117 B
RUSSIAN-OLIVE
Elaeagnus angustifolia
Zones 2–7
Potentially Invasive
See page 141
A culprit on the nation's Least Wanted list of invasive species
117 C
CALIFORNIA REDBUD, WESTERN REDBUD
Cercis orbiculata
Zones 7–9
Like its eastern relative, this small tree heralds the approach of Spring with beautiful pink blossoms along twigs and even parts of its trunk
117 D
NETLEAF HACKBERRY
Celtis reticulata
Zones 4–9
Twisted, tangled branches are ideal nesting places for a variety of birds

Are the lower leaf surfaces covered with golden scales; the fruit a 1–1½" (2.5–3.8 cm) bur with 1–2 nuts inside? It is a **giant golden chinkapin.**

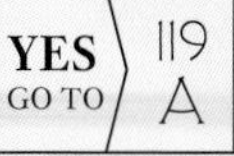

OR

Are the lower leaf surfaces not covered with golden scales; and the fruit fleshy, not bur-like?

Is the fruit 1" (2.5 cm) in diameter, greenish to purple, and olive-like; leaves always ENTIRE? **CLUE:** *The leaves are spicy-scented when crushed.* It is a **California bay laurel (Oregon myrtlewood).**

OR

Is the fruit a ⅓–½" (0.8–1.3 cm) long, orange berry; leaves occasionally TOOTHED on vigorously growing shoots?

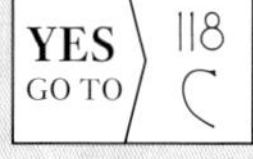

Is the bark thin and papery with a very distinctive red to red-brown color; the fruit covered with small bumps? **CLUE:** *Native along the Pacific coast from California to British Columbia.* It is a **Pacific madrone.**

OR

Is the bark gray; the fruit smooth? **CLUE:** *Native to southern Arizona and New Mexico.* It is an **Arizona madrone.**

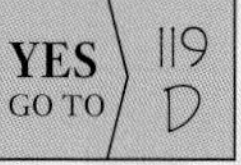

Do the leaves have flattened PETIOLES?

OR

Do the leaves not have flattened PETIOLES?

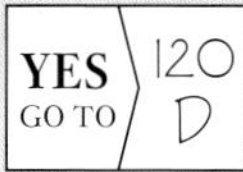

119 A
GIANT GOLDEN CHINKAPIN
Chrysolepis chrysophylla
Zones 6–9
The yellowish undersides of the leaves give this beautiful tree its name.
119 B
CALIFORNIA BAY LAUREL, OREGON MYRTLEWOOD
Umbellularia californica
Zones 7–9
Called by some "the most valued and best publicized hardwood species in the western United States."
119 C
PACIFIC MADRONE
Arbutus menziesii
Zones 7–9
A handsome tree with its reddish, papery bark and 'evergreen' foliage
119 D
ARIZONA MADRONE
Arbutus arizonica
Zones 7–9
Barely a native – the natural range of this small tree in the U.S. is only in the southeast corner of Arizona and southwest corner of adjoining New Mexico

Are leaf bases rounded, leaf edges finely TOOTHED; and buds non-resinous? It is a **quaking aspen.**

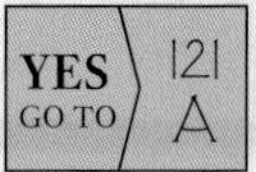

OR

Are leaf bases flat or angled, leaf edges finely or coarsely TOOTHED; and buds resinous?

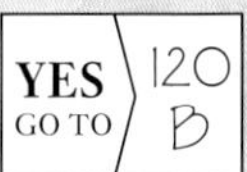

Does the tree have finely TOOTHED leaves and a column shape with branches reaching upward? **CLUE:** *This tree is widely used for shelterbelts and borders; sterile, it only occurs where planted.* It is a **Lombardy black poplar.**

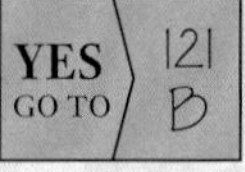

OR

Does the tree have coarsely TOOTHED leaves and not a column shape?

Do the leaves have 2 bumps where the leaf BLADE and PETIOLE meet? It is a **plains cottonwood.**

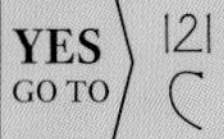

OR

Do the leaves not have bumps where the leaf BLADE and PETIOLE meet? It is a **Fremont cottonwood.**

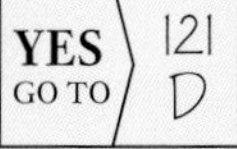

Do the leaves have 3–5 main veins extending from the base?

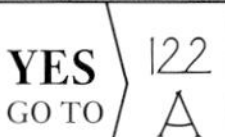

OR

Do the leaves have one MIDRIB extending from the base?

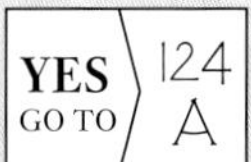

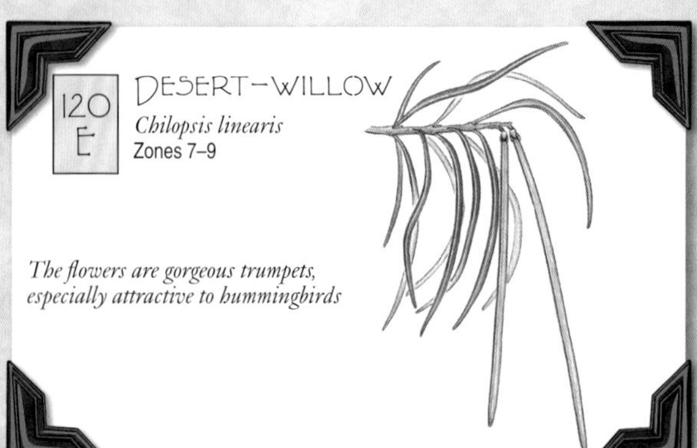

121 A QUAKING ASPEN

Populus tremuloides
Zones 2–7

Shaking in the slightest breeze and glorifying fall with its golden offering, quaking aspen beautifies more of North America than any other tree species

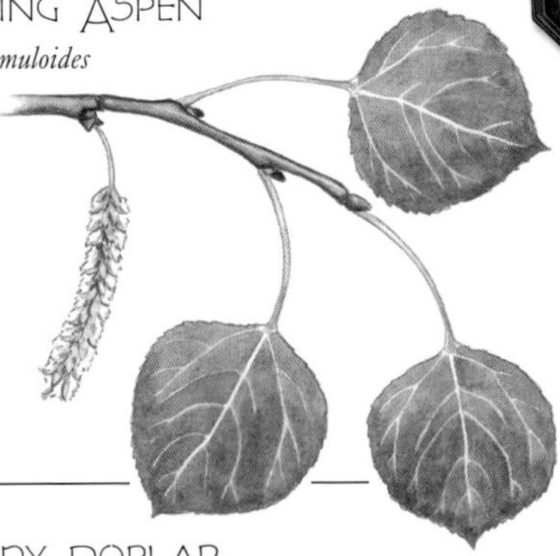

121 B LOMBARDY POPLAR

Populus nigra 'Italica'
Zones 3–9

'Instant shade'—tall, narrow and very fast-growing

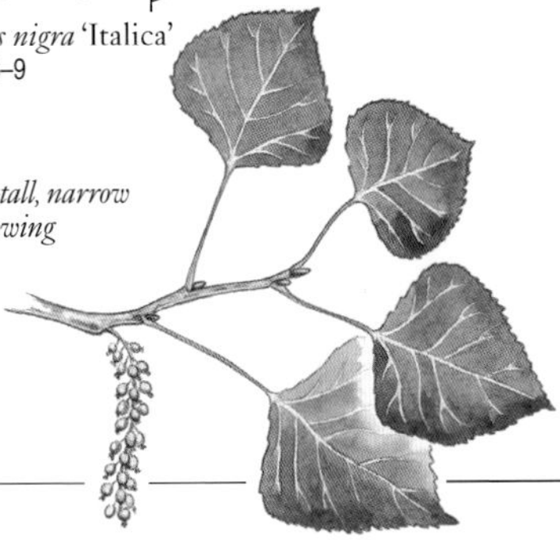

121 C PLAINS COTTONWOOD

Populus deltoides ssp. *monlifera*
Zones 3–9

"...shimmering, tremulous leaves (that) are hardly ever quiet, but if the wind stirs at all, rustle and quiver and sigh all day long..."

—Theodore Roosevelt, in Ranch Life and the Hunting Trail

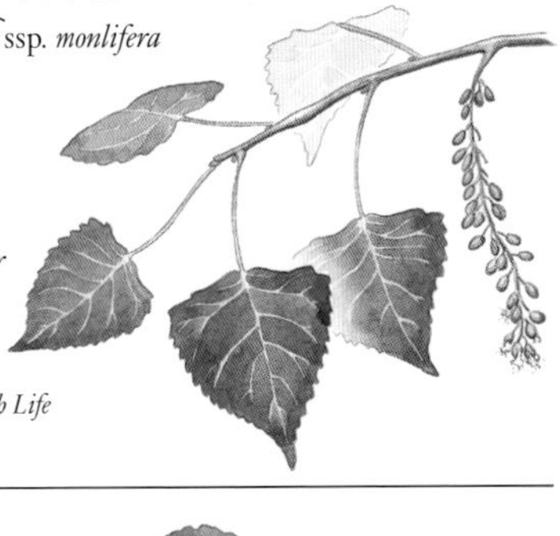

121 D FREMONT COTTONWOOD

Populus fremontii
Zones 5–9

Said to be a sacred tree to the Hopi Indians, with the wind in its quaking leaves being the voice of gods

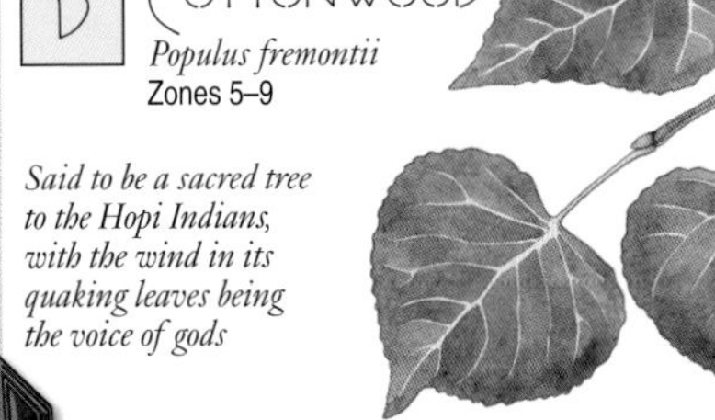

Are some leaves LOBED with leaf bases similar on both sides of the PETIOLE? **CLUE:** *The sap is milky; the fruit is fleshy and bumpy.* These are mulberry trees.

YES GO TO 122 B

OR

Are the leaf bases different on both sides of the PETIOLE? **CLUE:** *The sap is not milky; the fruit is not as above.*

YES GO TO 122 C

Are the leaves rough on top? **CLUE:** *Mature fruit (on the female tree) is red to dark purple.* It is a **red mulberry.**

YES GO TO 122 E

OR

Are the leaves smooth and glossy on top? **CLUE:** *Mature fruit (on the female tree) is white, pink or purple.* It is a **white mulberry.**

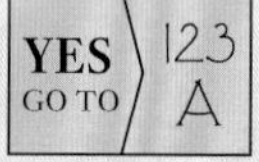

Are the leaves about twice as long as wide, tapered at the tip; bark has high, corky ridges? **CLUE:** *The fruit is purple and berry-like.* It is a **hackberry.**

YES GO TO 123 B

OR

Are the leaves heart-shaped and about as wide as long? **CLUE:** *The fruit is small and nut-like, attached to a wing-like leafy BRACT.* These are basswood or linden trees.

Are the leaves 5-6" (12.7–15.2 cm) long? It is an **American basswood (American linden).**

YES GO TO 123 C

OR

Are the leaves 1½–2½" (3.8–6.4 cm) long? It is a **littleleaf linden.**

YES GO TO 123 D

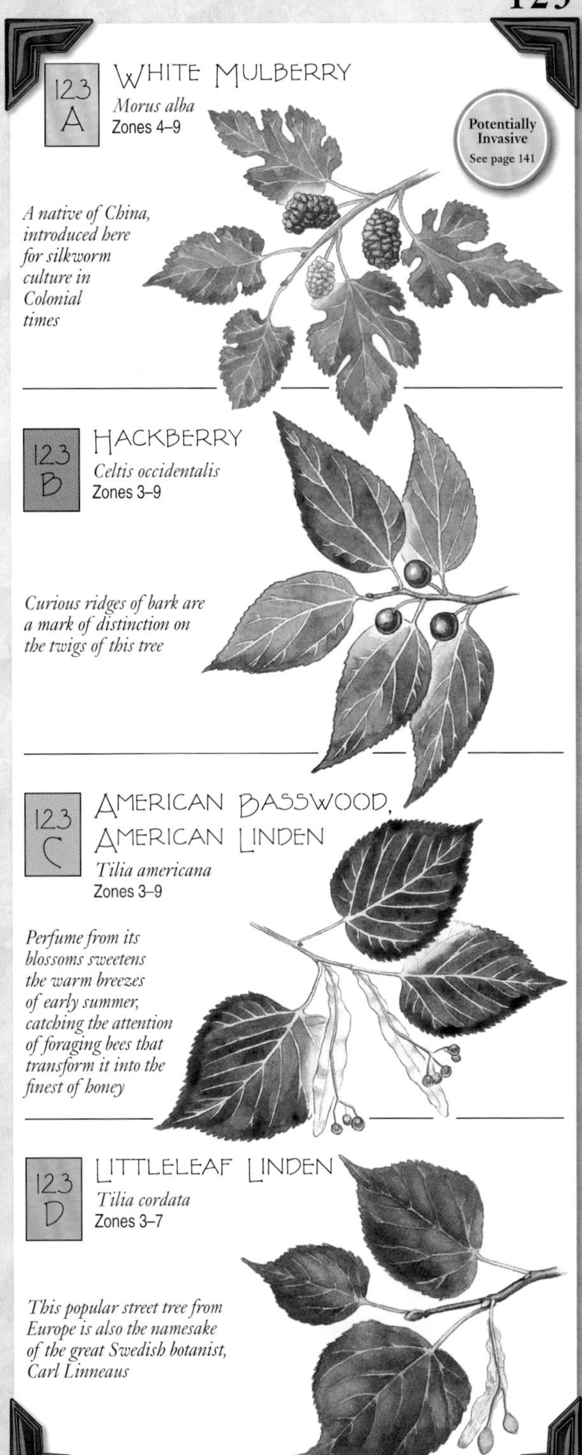
123 A
WHITE MULBERRY
Morus alba
Zones 4–9
Potentially Invasive
See page 141
A native of China, introduced here for silkworm culture in Colonial times
123 B
HACKBERRY
Celtis occidentalis
Zones 3–9
Curious ridges of bark are a mark of distinction on the twigs of this tree
123 C
AMERICAN BASSWOOD, AMERICAN LINDEN
Tilia americana
Zones 3–9
Perfume from its blossoms sweetens the warm breezes of early summer, catching the attention of foraging bees that transform it into the finest of honey
123 D
LITTLELEAF LINDEN
Tilia cordata
Zones 3–7
This popular street tree from Europe is also the namesake of the great Swedish botanist, Carl Linneaus

124

Is the fruit small, woody, and cone-like, with buds on stalks? These are alder trees.

YES GO TO 124 B

OR

Is the fruit not small, woody, and cone-like, with buds not stalked?

YES GO TO 126 A

Is the leaf MARGIN turned under and distinctively doubly TOOTHED? **CLUE:** *The small nuts in the fruit have a distinctive wing.* It is a **red alder.**

YES GO TO 125 A

OR

Is the leaf MARGIN not turned under and either singly or doubly TOOTHED? **CLUE:** *The small nuts in the fruit do not have a distinctive wing.*

Are the leaves thin; buds ¼-⅓" (0.6–0.8 cm) long and bright red? It is a **thinleaf alder (mountain alder).**

YES GO TO 125 B

OR

Are the leaves thicker and covered with small bumps; buds ½" (1.3 cm) long and dark red?

Are the leaves usually singly TOOTHED, with an oval-shaped leaf base? **CLUE:** *This tree is native from western Idaho, west to Washington, south through California.* It is a **white alder.**

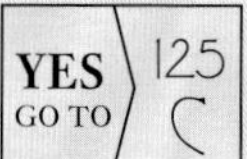

OR

Are the leaves usually doubly TOOTHED with a V-shaped leaf base? **CLUE:** *This tree is native to Arizona, southern New Mexico, and Mexico.* It is an **Arizona alder.**

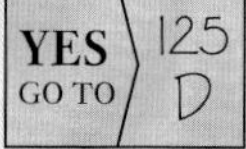

125 A
RED ALDER
Alnus rubra
Zones 5–9
The most abundant hardwood tree in the rainy Northwest
125 B
THINLEAF ALDER, MOUNTAIN ALDER
Alnus incana ssp. *tenuifolia*
Zones 2–7
Once the source of strong wood for bows and snowshoes
125 C
WHITE ALDER
Alnus rhombifolia
Zones 5–9
Flyfishers' nightmare along streams where it is usually at home
125 D
ARIZONA ALDER
Alnus oblongifolia
Zones 6–9
A little tree of moist sites in the dry Southwest—and able to add nitrogen to the soil through bacteria in nodules on its roots

Are the leaf bases different on both sides of the PETIOLE; leaves flattened horizontally along the twig? These are elm trees.

OR

Are the leaf bases the same on both sides of the PETIOLE?

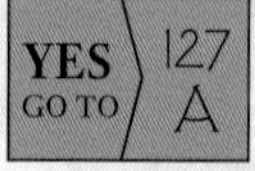

Are the leaves ¾–3" (1.9–7.6 cm) long, with singly TOOTHED MARGINS? **CLUE:** *Their bases may be only slightly different on both sides of the PETIOLE.* It is a **Siberian elm.**

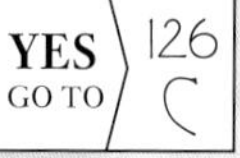

OR

Are the leaves 3–7" (7.6–17.8 cm) long, with doubly TOOTHED MARGINS?

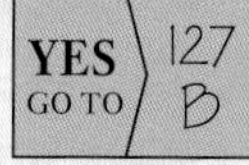

Are the leaves not over 4" (10.2 cm) long; do many of the twigs have corky wings or ridges? It is a **rock elm (cork elm).**

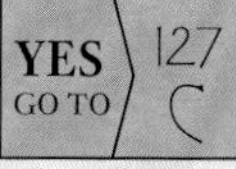

OR

Are the leaves over 4" (10.2 cm) long; do the twigs not have corky wings or ridges? It is an **American elm.**

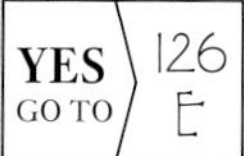

Is the bark on the trunk smooth, white to bronze color, and on some species papery and peeling easily? These are birch trees.

OR

Is the bark on the trunk not like above?

YES GO TO 128 B

Is the bark on older trunks and branches smooth and bronze colored and not peeling? It is a **water birch (red birch).**

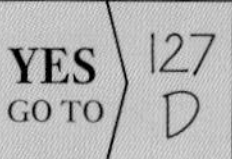

OR

Is the bark on older trunks and branches bright white with black cracks, peeling, and papery?

127 A SIBERIAN ELM

Ulmus pumila
Zones 4–9

Potentially Invasive
See page 141

Fast growing and disease resistant, but also considered an invasive species

---

127 B ROCK ELM, CORK ELM

Ulmus thomasii
Zones 3–7

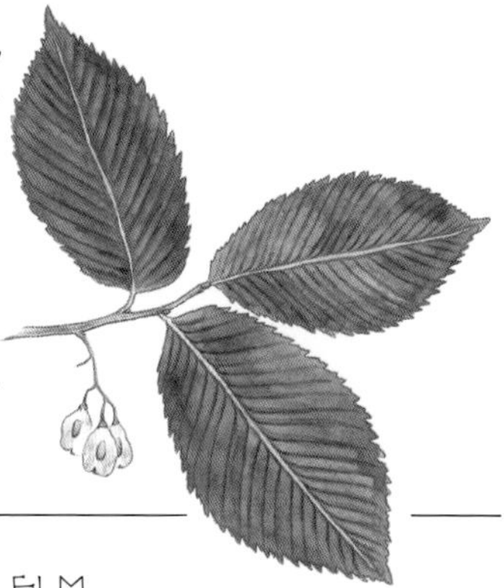

Two well deserved names—rock elm for its very hard wood, and cork elm for the corky wings on older branches

---

127 C AMERICAN ELM

Ulmus americana
Zones 3–9

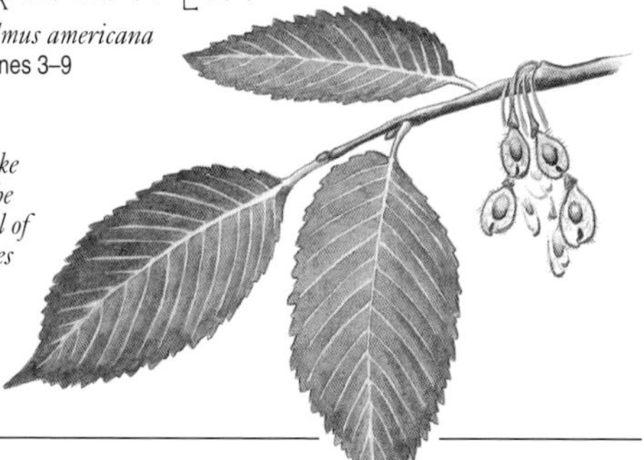

Its arching branches make this one of the most graceful of all shade trees

---

127 D WATER BIRCH, RED BIRCH

Betula occidentalis
Zones 4–6

"...also a small species of birch in but small quantities, the leaf of which is oval, finely indented, small and of a deep green colour."

—Meriwether Lewis, Jefferson River in Montana, August 3, 1805

Are the young twigs hairy and the branches erect? **CLUE:** *This tree is native across northern North America.* It is a **paper birch.**

YES GO TO 129 A

OR

Are the young twigs not hairy and the branches often droopy? **CLUE:** *This tree is not native across northern North America.* It is a **European white birch.**

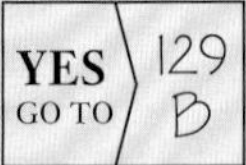

---

128 B

Is the fruit a small, dry CAPSULE containing hairy, tufted seeds?

OR

Is the fruit fleshy, not a CAPSULE?

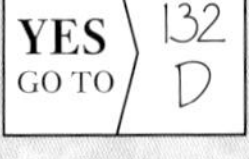

Do the twigs have a distinctive terminal (end) bud covered with several scales? These are cottonwood or poplar trees.

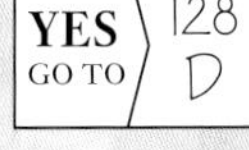

OR

Do the twigs have lateral buds covered with a single caplike scale? These are willow trees.

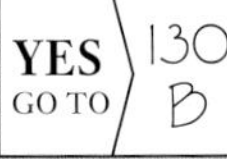

Is the PETIOLE less than one-third the length of the leaf BLADE; the leaves narrow? It is a **narrowleaf cottonwood.**

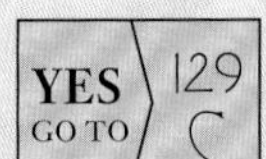

OR

Is the PETIOLE at least one half as long as the leaf BLADE; the leaves wide?

Are the leaves coarsely TOOTHED? **CLUE:** *The buds are ½–¾" (1.3–1.9 cm) long, slightly resinous, and aromatic.* It is a **lanceleaf cottonwood.**

OR

Are the leaves finely TOOTHED? **CLUE:** *The buds are ¾–1" (1.9–2.5 cm) long, very resinous, and aromatic.*

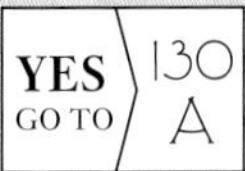

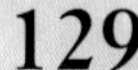

129 A — PAPER BIRCH

Betula papyrifera
Zones 2–7

The legendary white bark of birch canoes, lakeside vistas and beautiful lawns

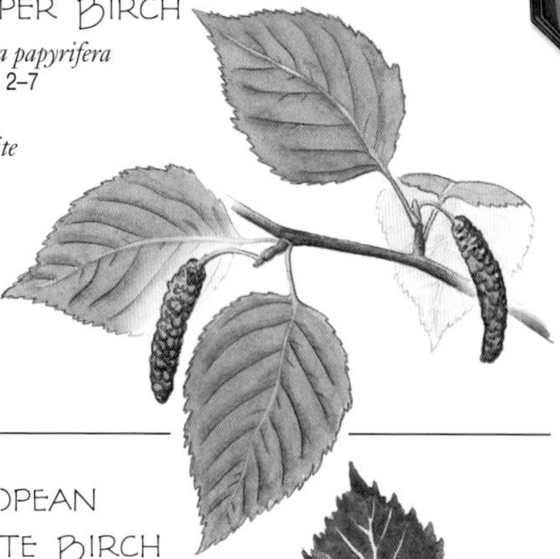

129 B — EUROPEAN WHITE BIRCH

Betula pendula
Zones 2–7

Graceful in summer and a dazzling display of bright yellow in autumn

129 C — NARROWLEAF COTTONWOOD

Populus angustifolia
Zones 3–9

Leaves like a willow, but not always; they vary a lot even on the same tree

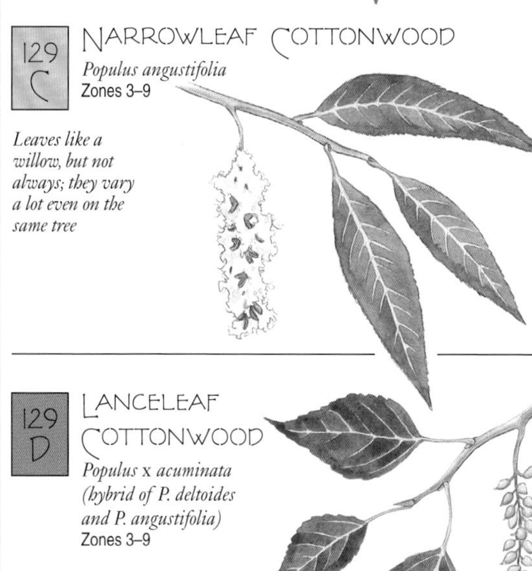

129 D — LANCELEAF COTTONWOOD

Populus x *acuminata*
(hybrid of P. deltoides and P. angustifolia)
Zones 3–9

Noted for its long leaf stem and spearhead-shaped leaves

Are the leaves only slightly longer than wide; with a hairy CAPSULE that is divided into three parts? **CLUE:** *This tree is native to the Pacific coast region and into Idaho and Montana.* It is a **black cottonwood.**

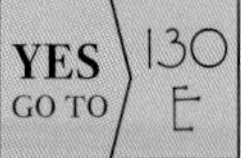

OR

Are the leaves about twice as long as wide, with a two-part CAPSULE that is not hairy? **CLUE:** *This tree is native across the northern U.S. and Canada.* It is a **balsam poplar.**

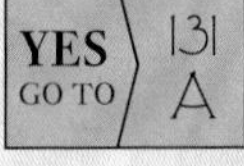

Are some mature leaves ENTIRE, with others very finely TOOTHED? **CLUE:** *The underside of the leaf is whitish-waxy and sometimes densely hairy.* It is a **Scouler's willow.**

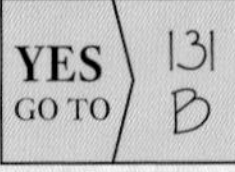

OR

Are all mature leaves coarsely or finely TOOTHED?

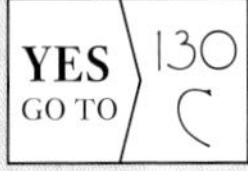

Does the PETIOLE have bumps near the base of the leaf BLADE?

OR

Does the PETIOLE not have bumps near the base of the leaf BLADE?

Are the leaves coarsely TOOTHED? **CLUE:** *Native to Europe and Asia, not the U.S., but has become naturalized in many areas of the western U.S.* It is a **crack willow.**

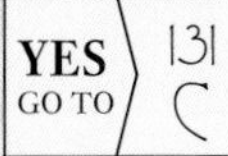

OR

Are the leaves finely TOOTHED? **CLUE:** *This tree is native to the western U.S. and Canada.* It is a **Pacific willow (yellow willow).**

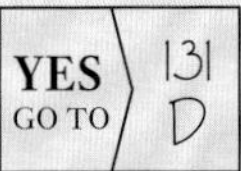

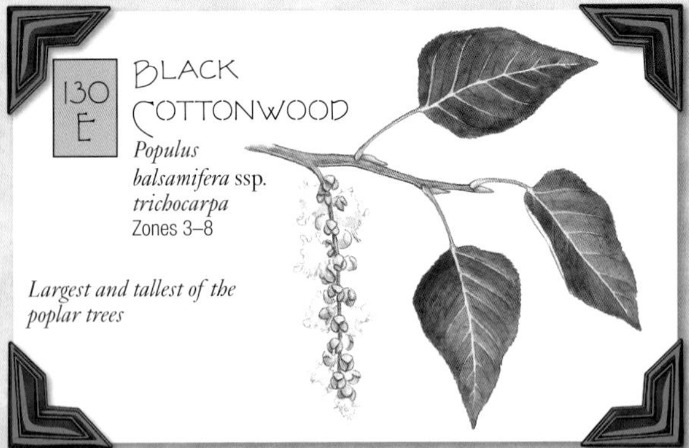

131 A BALSAM POPLAR

Populus balsamifera
Zones 2–5

Pleasing fragrance and growth that approaches 2 feet per year

131 B SCOULER'S WILLOW

Salix scouleriana
Zones 3–9

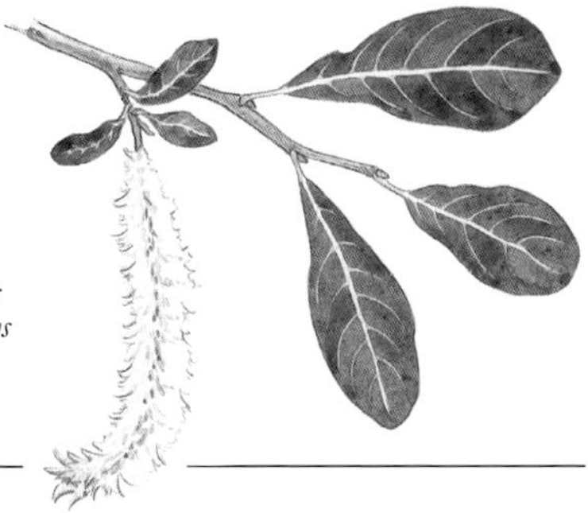

Found from Alaska to New Mexico, like other willows it had a wide variety of household uses and medicines in the days of pre-settlement

131 C CRACK WILLOW

Salix fragilis
Zones 3–9

When its branches break – which they do easily – listen for the loud 'crack'

131 D PACIFIC WILLOW, YELLOW WILLOW

Salix lucinda ssp. *lasiandra*
Zones 3–9

Spanning from Alaska to New Mexico, its inner bark provided early Americans with the equivalent of aspirin; it continues its usefulness today in windbreaks and stream bank stabilization

Are the leaves green on top and bottom surfaces? It is **Goodding's willow.**

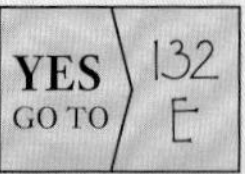

OR

Are the leaves green on the top surface; pale and sometimes waxy on the bottom?

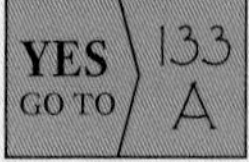

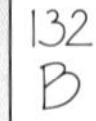

Are the older twigs olive-green to greenish brown? **CLUE:** *This tree is not native to the U.S., but is planted in the Southwest; it has a distinctive rounded crown.* It is a **globe Navajo willow (Hankow willow).**

OR

Are the older twigs red-brown to orange-brown? **CLUE:** *These trees are native to the U.S.*

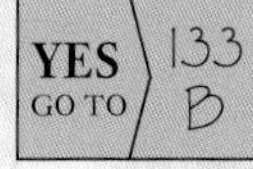

Are the twigs easily separated from the branches? **CLUE:** *Native throughout much of the Rocky Mountain region, Canada, and the upper Midwest.* It is a **peachleaf willow.**

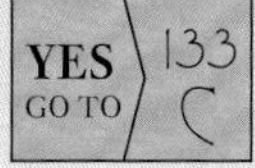

OR

Are the twigs not easily separated from the branches? **CLUE:** *This tree is native to the Southwest and much of California.* It is a **red willow.**

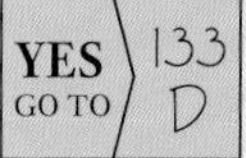

Are the leaves thick, spiny TOOTHED, and EVERGREEN? **CLUE:** *This tree is native to California; fruit is a fleshy, ¾–1¼" (1.9–3.2 cm), single-seeded cherry.* It is a **hollyleaf cherry.**

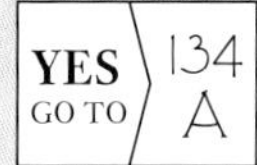

OR

Are the leaves thin, not spiny TOOTHED, and DECIDUOUS?

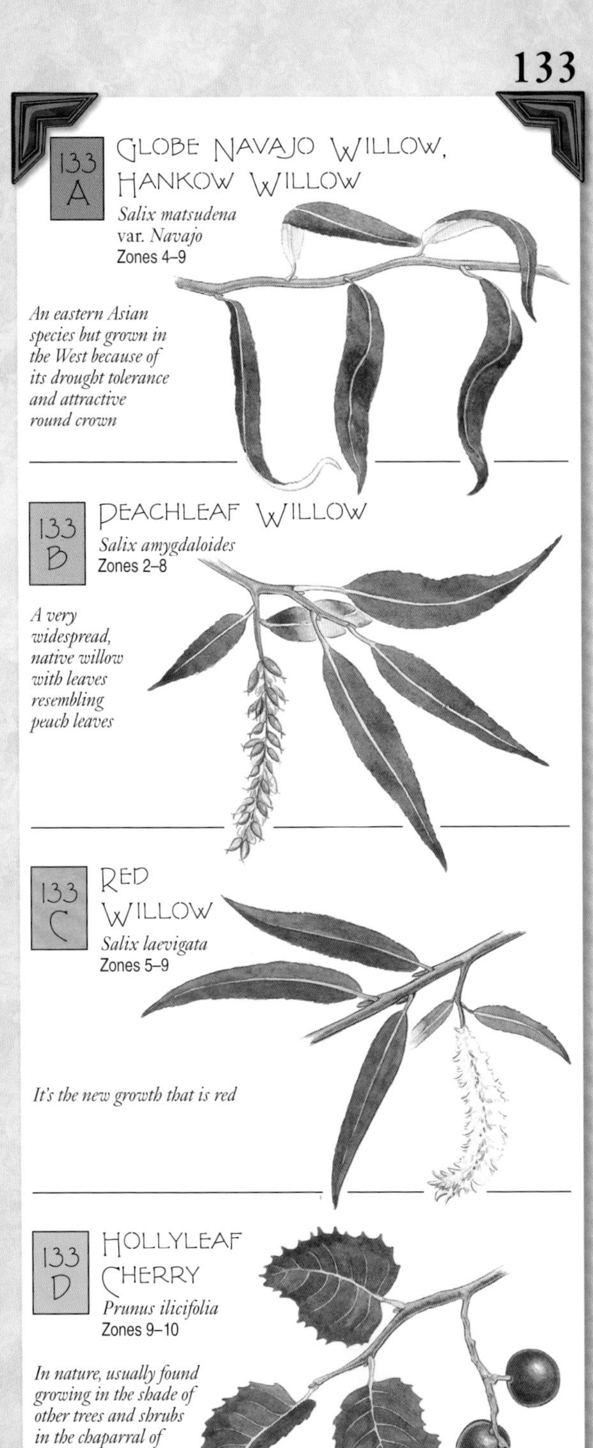

133 A — GLOBE NAVAJO WILLOW, HANKOW WILLOW

Salix matsudena var. *Navajo*
Zones 4–9

An eastern Asian species but grown in the West because of its drought tolerance and attractive round crown

133 B — PEACHLEAF WILLOW

Salix amygdaloides
Zones 2–8

A very widespread, native willow with leaves resembling peach leaves

133 C — RED WILLOW

Salix laevigata
Zones 5–9

It's the new growth that is red

133 D — HOLLYLEAF CHERRY

Prunus ilicifolia
Zones 9–10

In nature, usually found growing in the shade of other trees and shrubs in the chaparral of southern California

Do the twigs have buds that are covered with several scales, and fruit that is an apple or single-seeded cherry?

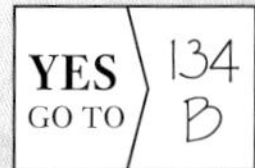

OR

Do the twigs have buds that are hairy and without scales? Fruit is a black, fleshy berry ⅓–½" (0.8–1.3 cm) in diameter with 2 to 3 seeds. It is a **Cascara buckthorn.**

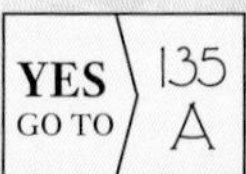

Is the fruit an apple, much more than ½" (1.3 cm) in diameter? It is an **apple.**

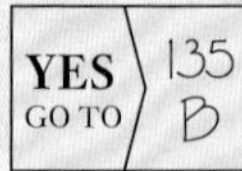

OR

Is the fruit a cherry, less than ½" (1.3 cm) in diameter? It is a **chokecherry.**

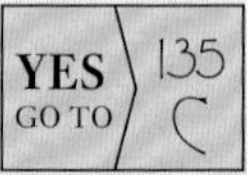

Are the leaves once PINNATELY COMPOUND?

OR

Are the leaves two or three times PINNATELY COMPOUND? (Paloverde leaves may appear to be a pair of once-PINNATELY COMPOUND leaves joined at their bases.)

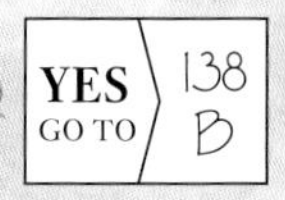

Is the fruit ¼–½" (0.6–1.3 cm) in diameter, bright orange-red, and berry-like? It is a **European mountainash.**

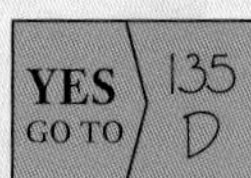

OR

Is the fruit a nut or a pod?

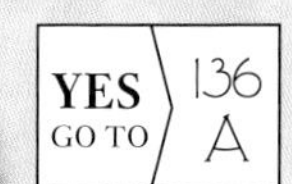

135 A — Cascara Buckthorn

Frangula purshiana
Zones 5–9

Indians alerted the Spanish missionaries to what is still a well-known use for this tree – constipation medicine made from its bark

135 B — Apple

Malus pumila (formerly *malus domestica)*
Zones 4–7

America's favorite fruit tree

135 C — Chokecherry

Prunus virginiana
Zones 2–9

A 'pioneer species' that thrives on the full sunshine of fencerows and abandoned fields

135 D — European Mountainash

Sorbus aucuparia
Zones 3–6

A deep freeze makes its pretty red fruits more palatable to birds

136

Is the fruit a nut?

OR

Is the fruit a LEGUME (a pod containing seeds)?

YES GO TO 136 D

Are there 15–23 leaf BLADES; nuts that are 1½–2" (3.8–5.1 cm) in diameter? **CLUE:** *Native to eastern Canada and U.S., this tree is planted in the West.* It is **black walnut.**

YES GO TO 137 A

OR

Are there 15 or less leaf BLADES (sometimes as many as 19); nuts that are 1½" (3.8 cm) or less in diameter? **CLUE:** *This tree is native to California or the Southwest.*

Is the fruit 1–1½" (2.5–3.8 cm) long, nut shell with shallow grooves, leaves with 9–13 BLADES (sometimes as many as 19)? **CLUE:** *This tree is native to Arizona, New Mexico, and Colorado.* It is an **Arizona walnut.**

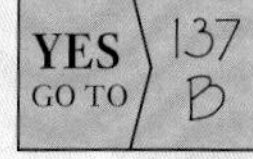

OR

Is the fruit ½–¾" (1.3–1.9 cm) long, nut shell with deep grooves, leaves with 9–15 BLADES (sometimes as many as 17)? **CLUE:** *Tree is native to California.* It is a **southern California walnut.**

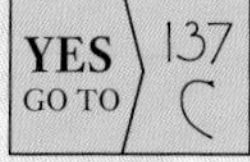

Are the leaf BLADES less than ½–¾" (1.3–1.9 cm) long, and the flowers purple? It is a **desert ironwood.**

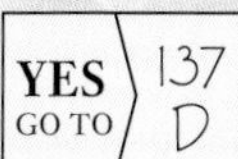

OR

Are the leaf BLADES more than 1" (2.5 cm) long; the flowers pink to white?

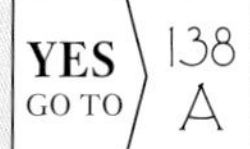

Black Walnut

Juglans nigra
Zones 4–9

Gunstocks, furniture and favorite nuts – this tree was a boon to the pioneers and is one of our most valuable trees today

Arizona Walnut

Juglans major
Zones 7–9

The only walnut to occur in desert conditions; and although only a small tree, its wood is every bit as beautiful as its larger cousins

Southern California Walnut

Juglans californica
Zones 8–9

Endemic to the riparian woodlands of California's lower elevation mountain ranges; usually no more than a shrub

Desert Ironwood

Olneya tesota
Zones 8–9

A resident of canyons in the Sonoran Desert – and called ironwood with wood so dense it sinks in water

138

Does each leaf contain 9–15 leaf BLADES; are the twigs covered with bumps? **CLUE:** *This tough tree is not native. Planted for its pale pink flowers.* It is a **New Mexican locust.**

YES GO TO 138 E

OR

Does each leaf contain 13–21 leaf BLADES; are the twigs covered with sticky bumps? **CLUE:** *This tree is not native to the western U.S.* It is an **Idaho flowering locust.**

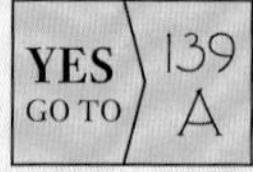

Are the leaf BLADES ½" (1.3 cm) or longer?

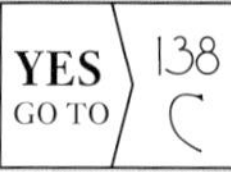

OR

Are the leaf BLADES ⅓" (0.8 cm) or less?

Are the leaf BLADES 2–2½" (5.1–6.4 cm) long, with pointed, angled tips; the seeds ½–¾" (1.3–1.9 cm) long? **CLUE:** *This tree is not native to the West.* It is a **Kentucky coffeetree.**

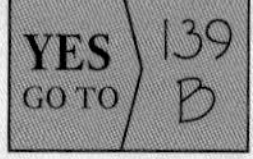

OR

Are the leaf BLADES ½–2" (1.3–5.1 cm) long, with rounded tips; the seeds ⅓" (0.8 cm) long or less?

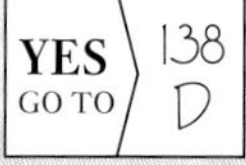

Are the twigs armed with sharp spines ½–2" (1.3–5.1 cm) long; the 4–9" (10.2–22.9 cm) pod does not split lengthwise along 2 lines? **CLUE:** *This tree is native throughout the Southwest.* It is a **mesquite.**

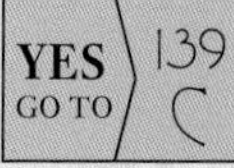

OR

Are the twigs not armed with sharp spines, though some trees may have branched thorns on branches and the trunk; the 12–18" (30.5–45.7 cm) pod splits lengthwise along 2 lines? **CLUE:** *This tree is not native to the western U.S.* It is a **honeylocust.**

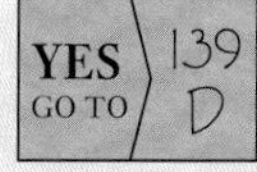

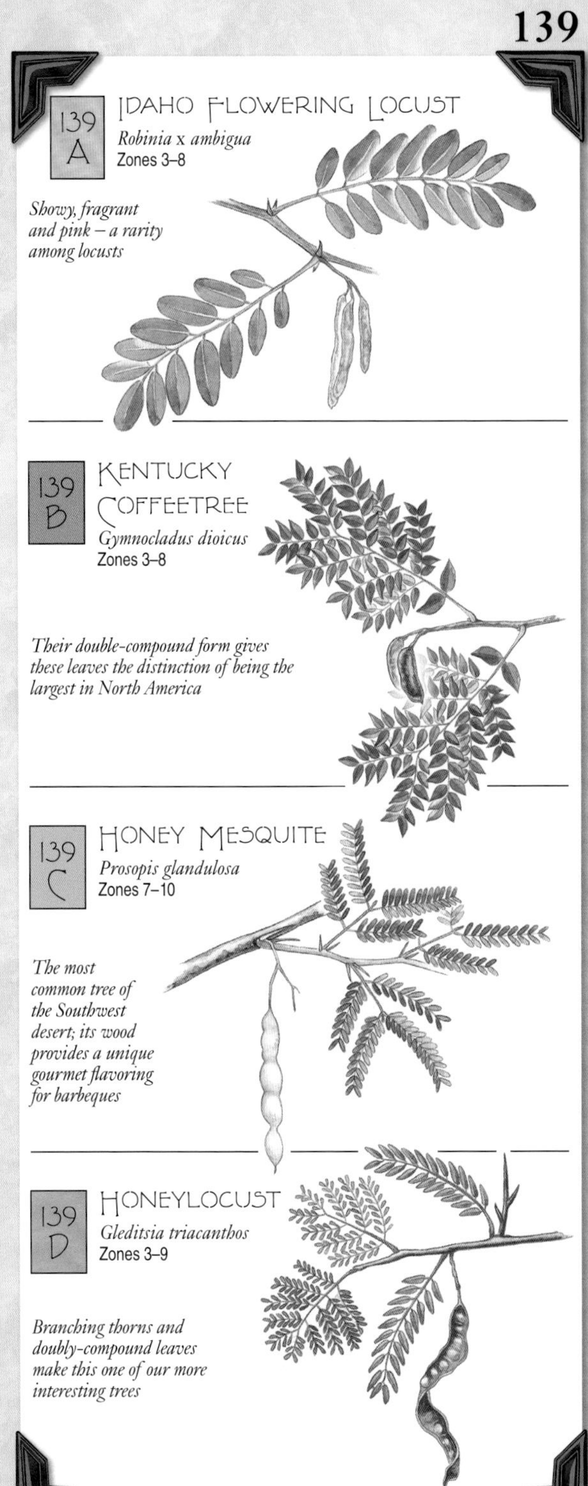

139 A

Idaho Flowering Locust

Robinia x ambigua
Zones 3–8

Showy, fragrant and pink – a rarity among locusts

139 B

Kentucky Coffeetree

Gymnocladus dioicus
Zones 3–8

Their double-compound form gives these leaves the distinction of being the largest in North America

139 C

Honey Mesquite

Prosopis glandulosa
Zones 7–10

The most common tree of the Southwest desert; its wood provides a unique gourmet flavoring for barbeques

139 D

Honeylocust

Gleditsia triacanthos
Zones 3–9

Branching thorns and doubly-compound leaves make this one of our more interesting trees

140

Are the leaves 6–18" (15.2–45.7 cm) long with 40–60 leaf BLADES; the leaves stay on the tree until fall? It is a **Jerusalem-thorn.**

YES GO TO 140 C

OR

Are the leaves 2" (5.1 cm) or less with 4–12 leaf BLADES; the leaves fall off quickly, but sometimes resprout with late summer rains?

YES GO TO 140 B

Are there 4–6 leaf BLADES; a pod that has 2–8 seeds? It is a **blue paloverde.**

YES GO TO 140 D

OR

Are there 8–12 leaf BLADES; a pod that has 1–2 seeds? It is a **yellow paloverde.**

YES GO TO 140 E

---

140 C

JERUSALEM-THORN

Parkinsonia aculeata

Zones 9–10

Portions of old leaves cling like leathery streamers, making this an interesting addition to a cactus garden or Xeriscape landscape

---

140 D

BLUE PALOVERDE

Parkinsonia florida

Zones 8–10

Along with the other member of this genus, yellow paloverde, it shares the honor of being Arizona's state tree

---

140 E

YELLOW PALOVERDE

Parkinsonia microphylla

Zones 9–10

Arizona's state tree and a master of desert survival; when its leaves are shed due to drought, its green twigs and trunk continue photosynthesis

This symbol indicates that a tree is potentially invasive.

Invasive plants are known to reproduce rapidly and quickly spread over large areas of land. They have few natural controls such as herbivores or diseases to stop their spread and they can threaten biological diversity.

Contact your local County Cooperative Extension Agent or State Forester to learn about invasive trees and plants in your area.

89B
TAMARISK,
SALTCEDAR
Tamarix chinensis

97A
AMUR MAPLE,
GINNALA MAPLE
Acer ginnala

105A
WHITE POPLAR
Populus alba

109B, 123A
WHITE MULBERRY
Morus alba

117B
RUSSIAN OLIVE
Elaeagnus angustifolia

127A
SIBERIAN ELM
Ulmus pumila

INDEX

INDEX (CONTINUED)

INDEX (CONTINUED)

INDEX (CONTINUED)

INDEX (CONTINUED)

INDEX (CONTINUED)

INDEX (CONTINUED)

HOW TO ORDER

The **What Tree Is That?** tree identification booklet can be purchased in quantities with generous discounts—ideal for students, nature centers, garden clubs, or community events.

Online ordering is easy at **arborday.org/whattree** or call Member Services at the Arbor Day Foundation at 1-888-448-7337.

ARBORDAY.ORG

You can also find a fun, interactive version of this **What Tree Is That?** tree identification guide online at **arborday.org/whattree**. With a leaf in hand, simply click through the steps to find out the species.

MOBILE

You can also use the **What Tree Is That?** identification guide on your smart phone at **arborday.org/smarttree**. It's easy, convenient, and free!

Arborday.org & Smart Phones

You can also find a free, interactive version of this **What Tree Is That?** tree identification guide online at **arborday.org/smarttree**. With a leaf in hand, simply click though the steps to find out the species.

iPhone & iPad

Visit iTunes for the **What Tree Is That?** identification guide at **arborday.org/iphone**. This app keeps track of the trees you've identified using the GPS and mapping functionality integrated into your iPhone or iPad.

PLANT TREES!

Many of the species identified in this booklet are available and affordably priced from the Arbor Day Foundation. Your trees will be shipped at the right time for planting in your area with planting instructions. Shopping is easy and convenient at **arborday.org/treestore**.

MORE INFORMATION

You can learn much more about each tree species at **arborday.org/treeguide**. Find out how to plant and care for a tree, its growth rate, soil and sun preference, and thorough descriptions of its uses and historic importance.

FIELD NOTES

FIELD SKETCHES

FIELD NOTES

FIELD SKETCHES

Field Notes

FIELD SKETCHES

FIELD NOTES

The Benefits of Becoming a Member

You can join the Arbor Day Foundation for only $10 and get:

1) 10 Free Trees

Your 6"–12" trees will arrive at the best time for planting in your area. To see the choices available in your hardiness zone or to give a gift membership, visit **arborday.org**.

2) Tree Discounts

You'll also receive a 33-56 percent discount on over 100 trees and shrubs. Our selection includes shade, flowering, ornamental, fruit trees, evergreens and more.

3) *Arbor Day* Subscription

Free subscription to our colorful bimonthly newsletter. *Arbor Day* is a gardener's handbook and tree information guide in one.

4) The Tree Book

The Tree Book is a treasury of genuinely useful guidance about planting and caring for trees in a cheerfully colorful format.

5) Six Month or One Year Membership

Important Arbor Day Foundation programs are supported by nearly a million members nationwide. You'll become part of the Foundation.

FIELD SKETCHES